GETTING TO KNOW THE
HOLY SPIRIT
STUDY GUIDE

What the Bible says about the Holy Spirit and why it matters to you

Susan Wedeking Gregory
David Gregory

GETTING TO KNOW THE HOLY SPIRIT STUDY GUIDE
WHAT THE BIBLE SAYS ABOUT THE HOLY SPIRIT AND WHY IT MATTERS TO YOU

Credits
Designer: Susan Wedeking Gregory
Copy Editor: Dana Monroe Samson

Published in Evansville, Indiana, by Vortex Publishing

Scripture quotations marked NIV are taken from the Holy Bible, New International Version®, NIV®. Copyright © 1973, 1978, 1984, 2011 by Biblica, Inc.™ Used by permission. All rights reserved worldwide.

Scripture quotations marked NASB are taken from the New American Standard Bible® (NASB), Copyright © 1960, 1962, 1963, 1968, 1971, 1972, 1973, 1975, 1977, 1995 by The Lockman Foundation. Used by permission. www.Lockman.org

Scripture quotations marked KJV are from the King James Version of the Bible.

ISBN 978-0-9966959-1-6 (Paperback)

Printed in the United States of America

For Andrea and Brandon

Contents

Preface

Who is the Holy Spirit? What is His role in the Trinity? Why did Jesus, on the night before He died, tell the disciples that He would ask the Father to send the Holy Spirit? What does that mean, and what does it have to do with you?

These and many other questions about the Holy Spirit are addressed in this study guide. Everything in this book is based on the Holy Bible (Old and New Testaments), what it teaches us about the Holy Spirit, and why it's important for us to get to know Him better.

This study guide explores forty-eight ministries of the Holy Spirit, grouped into twelve lessons, and how they apply to your everyday life. This study will help you identify how the Holy Spirit is already at work in your life, and it offers tools on how to be more intentional in allowing Him to direct your daily activities.

The information in this study guide is based on Christianity, but it is not affiliated with any particular denomination or organization. It is intended for those who seek to better understand the Holy Spirit and develop a deeper relationship with God.

The concept for this study guide developed during the writing of our previous book, *Vortex of the Holy Spirit: Finding Supernatural Love After Superstorm Sandy*, an amazing true story about how the Holy Spirit drew people together to help each other in the wake of the storm in 2012.

After this experience, we realized that we had an inaccurate concept of who the Holy Spirit is. We felt an overwhelming desire to learn more about Him and started an intensive study about how He works in all of our lives. When we spoke with others about the Holy Spirit, the response was often "I don't really know that much about the Holy Spirit." The research we had begun during that study ended up changing our lives, so we decided to compile it in an organized way. This study guide is the result of that work.

Great care has been taken to reflect what the Bible teaches about the Holy Spirit, and this study guide has been reviewed by several well-educated, committed Christians who have a high view of Scripture.

While this study guide covers forty-eight ministries of the Holy Spirit, this is not to imply that it covers everything He does; these are simply the topics that we have chosen to focus on for this study. Nor is it to imply that we have everything figured out about the Holy Spirit; in fact, quite the opposite is true. The search for knowledge about God—and developing a deeper relationship with Him—is a lifelong adventure.

We hope you'll join us on the journey.

Susan and David

How to Use This Study Guide

This study guide is designed to be used as a twelve-lesson curriculum, ideal for Sunday school classes or small groups. If you are studying by yourself, you can simply go through the material at your own pace. Either way, the Holy Spirit will be there to help you!

Teaching Outline

The structure of this study guide is part Bible study and part life application. The goal is to become more familiar with what the Bible says about the Holy Spirit and how that information directly affects your life.

Because this is a study on the Holy Spirit, scriptures are taken from several books in the Bible and are grouped in ways that support the overall theme of each of the twelve lessons.

Every lesson includes four topically related main scriptures, each one covering a ministry of the Holy Spirit. Each ministry has a brief explanation and questions for reflection and discussion.

Depending on how your group is organized, you can have one leader for the entire study guide or assign lessons to different people to lead.

Here are some tips for using this study guide:

1. Pray before and after each time you explore the information in this book. Prior to each study session, along with whatever God is prompting, we encourage you to pray for discernment and that the Holy Spirit will open your eyes, ears, and heart to what He is saying to you. Also pray that the scriptures will come alive in you in a new and powerful way. Afterwards, thank God for your new understanding, and ask that the meaning of what you have learned will deepen as you continue to reflect on the information.

2. The original language of the New Testament is Greek, and in some instances, a more in-depth translation of key words can be helpful. In such cases, the Greek word is cited along with the reference for its definition (Strong's XXXX). This citation refers to information found in *Strong's Exhaustive Concordance of the Bible* and *AMG's Annotated Strong's Dictionaries.*

3. Look up the scriptural cross references to enhance your understanding and context for the main verse. One of the wonderful things about the Bible is that most verses relate to other verses. Going back and forth between related scriptures often results in a more thorough understanding of each verse.

4. This is your study guide—feel free to write, underline, highlight, draw, doodle, or use whatever method you want to help you understand the information in this book. Ample room has been allocated for you to answer questions, make lists, jot down thoughts, etc.

Before You Begin

Before you begin this study, it is helpful to have a little background information about the Holy Spirit.

First of all, depending on which version of the Bible you use, the Holy Spirit is also known as the Holy Ghost. He's mentioned many times in both the Old and New Testaments and can be referred to as the Spirit of the LORD (Isa. 59:19), the Spirit of God, (1 Cor. 3:16), the Spirit of Christ (Rom. 8:9), the Spirit (John 3:5), the eternal Spirit (Heb. 9:14), the Spirit of truth (John 16:13), the Spirit of grace (Heb. 10:29), the Spirit of glory (1 Pet. 4:14), the Spirit of life (Rom. 8:2), and other names.

He's also part of the Trinity of God, which includes the Father, the Son, and the Holy Spirit (John 16:15). The thirteenth-century diagram below, known as the "Shield of the Trinity," is a simple, yet effective, way to illustrate this complex and often confusing relationship:

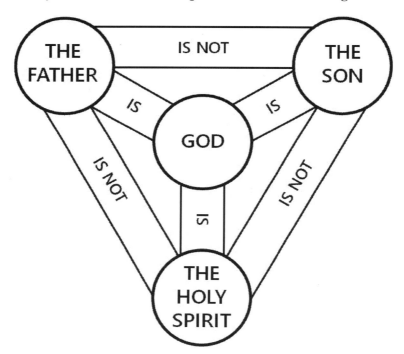

In addition, the Holy Spirit is the power behind many of the most significant events in the history of the earth including: the formation of the earth (Gen. 1:1–2); the birth of Jesus (Luke 1:35); the resurrection of Christ (Rom. 8:11); and the beginning of the Christian church (Acts 2:1–4).

He's still at work today indwelling believers and transforming their lives. If you've already met Him, He'd like to get to know you better. If not, He's hoping for the invitation to become part of your life.

All this I have spoken while still with you.
But the Advocate, the Holy Spirit, whom the
Father will send in my name, will teach you
all things and will remind you of everything
I have said to you.

(The words of Jesus as recorded in John 14:25–26, NIV)

1
THE HOLY SPIRIT

THE HOLY SPIRIT GUIDES US INTO TRUTH

But when he, the Spirit of truth, comes, he will guide you into all the truth. (John 16:13 NIV)

LEARNING THE SCRIPTURE

1. But when he, the _____ _____ _____ comes, he will _____

   you into _____ _____ _____.

GOING DEEPER

These words were written by the apostle John, who was a disciple of Jesus. John's gospel includes his eye-witness account of Jesus's life and ministry, several of His miracles, many of His teachings, and His death and resurrection. John said he wrote the gospel "that you may believe that Jesus is the Messiah, the Son of God, and that by believing you may have life in his name" (John 20:31 NIV).

John was present at the Last Supper. On that night, Jesus gathered with the disciples in the upper room to tell them that He would be leaving (John 13:1, Matt. 26:17–18). The unthinkable moment had arrived, and the disciples were filled with fear and sorrow.

To comfort them, Jesus told the disciples that He was sending someone else, the Holy Spirit, to help them after He was gone. "If you love me, keep my commands. And I will ask the Father, and he will give you another advocate to help you and be with you forever—the Spirit of truth" (John 14:15–17 NIV).

The Greek word for "advocate" is *paraklētos*, also meaning "counselor," "comforter," "intercessor," or "one called upon for help" (Strong's 3875).

The messenger of Christ's further revelation to the disciples would be the Spirit of truth, guiding them into all truth. The Holy Spirit, who inspired the writing of the Old Testament (2 Pet. 1:21) would also inspire the new one (1 Cor. 2:9–10).

Only the Holy Spirit, because He is God, knows everything that God knows, and so is able to reveal divine truth to man. "All that belongs to the Father is mine. That is why I said the Spirit will receive from me what he will make known to you" (John 16:15 NIV).

REFLECT

1. Where did the Last Supper take place?

2. Who is the Spirit of truth?

3. Read John 20:31. Why did John write this gospel? How is this significant to you? Discuss.

4. Write a prayer asking the Holy Spirit to guide you into all the truth as you strive to know Him better throughout this study guide.

THE HOLY SPIRIT GLORIFIES JESUS

When the Advocate comes, whom I will send to you from the Father—the Spirit of truth who goes out from the Father—he will testify about me. And you also must testify, for you have been with me from the beginning. (John 15:26–27 NIV)

He will glorify me because it is from me that he will receive what he will make known to you. (John 16:14 NIV)

LEARNING THE SCRIPTURE

1. When the _____ comes, whom I will _____ _____ _____ from the Father—the _____ _____ _____ who goes out from the Father—he will _____ about me. And _____ _____ must testify, for you have been with me from _____ _____.

2. He will _____ me because it is from me that he _____ _____ what he will _____ _____ to you.

GOING DEEPER

Jesus devoted His last night on earth to teaching the disciples, giving them final instructions, calming their fears, and assuring them of His continuing love for them (John chapters 13, 14, 15). Jesus also promised that He would send the Advocate—the Spirit of truth—who would testify about Him. Through the ministry of the Holy Spirit, Jesus would be glorified as the truth about Him is revealed through Scripture.

Jesus prayed for the disciples (John 17:9) and that future generations would believe, "I pray also for those who will believe in me through their [the disciples'] message" (v. 20 NIV, clarification added); He also prayed that they would know His glory, "Father, I want those you have given me to be with me where I am, and to see my glory" (v. 24 NIV).

Christians today are not eyewitnesses to the life of Jesus as the disciples were, but the Holy Spirit works to make Jesus known to a lost world, thereby leading all to salvation.

REFLECT

1. List some additional names for the "Advocate" in other places in the Bible and in other versions of the Bible. Hint: See John 15:26 and "Before You Begin" on page viii. (Compare different versions of the Bible at www.biblehub.com and www.biblegateway.com.)

2. How does the sending of the Holy Spirit enable Christ to reach people through the disciples? Through all believers? Explain.

3. What did Jesus instruct the disciples to do in John 15:27? How does this apply to you? Discuss.

THE HOLY SPIRIT DIRECTS US TO LIFE IN CHRIST

You, however, are not in the realm of the flesh but are in the realm of the spirit, if indeed the Spirit of God lives in you. And if anyone does not have the Spirit of Christ, they do not belong to Christ. (Rom. 8:9 NIV)

LEARNING THE SCRIPTURE

1. You, however, are _____ in the realm of the _____ but are in the realm of the spirit.

2. If indeed the _____ of God lives in you.

3. And if anyone does not have the Spirit of _____, they do not belong to _____.

GOING DEEPER

The book of Romans is a letter from Paul to the believers in Rome, hence the name "Romans." In it, Paul provided a theological foundation on which believers could build their faith and serve God effectively. Romans reveals the answers to important questions and provides information on many topics such as salvation, the sovereignty of God, judgment, spiritual growth, and the righteousness of God.

A common theme in Romans is the dichotomous issue of having a sinful nature or being directed by the Spirit of God. Paul expressed his own struggle between the spirit and flesh in Acts 7:21–25 (NIV): "So I find this law at work: Although I want to do good, evil is right there with me. For in my inner being I delight in God's law; but I see another law at work in me, waging war against the law of my mind and making me a prisoner of the law of sin at work within me. What a wretched man I am! Who will rescue me from this body that is subject to death? Thanks be to God, who delivers me through Jesus Christ our Lord!"

Paul says that if we are indwelled by the Holy Spirit, we belong to God. Not only that, he adds, "But if Christ is in you, then even though your body is subject to death because of sin, the Spirit gives life because of righteousness. And if the Spirit of him who raised Jesus from the dead is living in you, he who raised Christ from the dead will also give life to your mortal bodies because of his Spirit who lives in you" (Rom. 8:10–11 NIV).

REFLECT

1. Romans 8:9 mentions both the "Spirit of God" and the "Spirit of Christ." To whom are these referring? Explain.

2. Read Romans 8:10–11. What does Paul say about the body and the Spirit? Discuss.

3. Read Romans 8:21–25. What is Paul thankful for in his own struggle between Spirit and flesh? Discuss.

4. Paul struggled between flesh and Spirit. Do you have similar conflicts? How have you dealt with these conflicts thus far? Write down ways the Holy Spirit can help you with these conflicts going forward.

THE HOLY SPIRIT BEARS WITNESS ABOUT THE RESURRECTION OF JESUS CHRIST

We are witnesses of these things, and so is the Holy Spirit, whom God has given to those who obey him. (Acts 5:32 NIV)

LEARNING THE SCRIPTURE

1. We are _____ of these things, and so is the _____ _____,

2. Whom _____ has given to those who _____ him.

GOING DEEPER

The book of Acts was written by Luke, and, together with the gospel bearing his name, the two books span more than sixty years. Luke records details on the birth, life, death, resurrection, and ascension of Jesus; the coming of the Holy Spirit; the history of the early Christian church; and the actions of the apostles. Luke, who was a physician and Greek Christian, accompanied the apostle Paul on several mission journeys.

In Acts 5:17–20, Luke gives a description of a time after Jesus's resurrection when Peter and the other disciples had been arrested for preaching about Jesus. An angel of the Lord released the apostles from jail and instructed them to go to the temple courts and preach about a new life in Jesus.

When questioned by the Sanhedrin, the ruling Jewish council in Jerusalem, about why they continued to disobey the order not to talk about Jesus, the apostles indicated that they had witnessed the events they were declaring—and that they had to obey God rather than man (vv. 27–29).

When we receive the Holy Spirit at our salvation (Rom. 8:9, Acts 2:4, 1 Cor. 6:19 and 12:13), we, too, are witnesses to the resurrection of Christ through the revelation of God's Word through the Spirit. This understanding is foundational to our faith as Christians and gives us hope for eternal life.

REFLECT

1. Read Acts 5:29–32. How might the Holy Spirit have influenced Peter in verse 29? Discuss.

2. When Peter makes his final statement in Acts 5:32, does it seem like he is making a point directed at the Sanhedrin when he says: God gives the Holy Spirit to "those who obey him"? Discuss.

3. Read Mark 14:66–71. Compare Peter's actions the night before Jesus's crucifixion with his behavior as recorded in Acts. In Mark, Peter's faith was tested, and he failed. In Acts, his faith was tested, and he succeeded. Can the Holy Spirit strengthen your conviction in Christ as He did for Peter? Discuss.

2
THE HOLY SPIRIT

11

THE HOLY SPIRIT BAPTIZES US

For John baptized with water, but in a few days you will be baptized with the Holy Spirit. (Acts 1:5 NIV)

LEARNING THE SCRIPTURE

1. John baptized with _____, but in a few days, _____ will be _____

   with the _____ _____.

GOING DEEPER

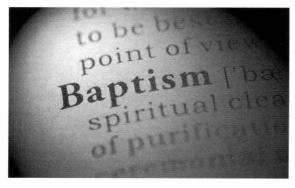

In the book of Acts 1:4–9, Luke records the final instructions Jesus gave to the disciples before He ascended into heaven. Jesus told the disciples to wait in Jerusalem "for the gift my Father promised," meaning the coming of the Holy Spirit at Pentecost (v. 4). On that day, the Holy Spirit was made available to all who believed in Jesus (Acts 2:38–39). We receive the Holy Spirit when we receive Jesus Christ at our salvation (Rom. 8:9, Acts 2:4, 1 Cor. 6:19 and 12:13).

Baptism with the Holy Spirit had been prophesied by John the Baptist: "As for me, I baptize you with water; but One is coming who is mightier than I, and I am not fit to untie the thong of His sandals; He will baptize you with the Holy Spirit and fire" (Luke 3:16–17 NASB).

John baptized with water, as a sign of penitence, in reference to the *remission* of sin; but Christ baptizes with the Holy Spirit for the *destruction* of sin, the illumination of the mind, and the consolation of the heart.

It was the coming of the gift of the Holy Spirit that enabled the disciples to become the first preachers of Christianity, establish churches throughout the region, withstand persecution, and record the New Testament for future generations.

When we are saved, the Holy Spirit is the power and guide of our new lives. He starts a lifelong process of change to help us become more like Christ (2 Cor. 3:18).

REFLECT

1. In Acts 1:4, what "gift" is promised?

2. To whom is the gift made available?

3. What action enables the Holy Spirit to come into our lives?

THE HOLY SPIRIT GIVES BIRTH TO OUR SPIRIT

Jesus answered, "Very truly I tell you, no one can enter the kingdom of God unless they are born of water and the Spirit. Flesh gives birth to flesh, but the Spirit gives birth to spirit." (John 3:5–6 NIV)

LEARNING THE SCRIPTURE

2. Jesus said, "Very truly I tell you, _____ _____ can _____ the kingdom of God unless they are born of _____ and the _____.

3. Flesh gives birth to _____, but the _____ gives birth to _____.

GOING DEEPER

Everyone wants to enter the Kingdom of God, so Jesus describes what is required in this verse. Being born of water and the Spirit is sometimes referred to as being "born again." "Water" and "Spirit" are used together in the following two scriptures—one each from the Old Testament and New Testament—to describe how they relate to salvation as depicted by Jesus:

1. "For I will take you out of the nations; I will gather you from all the countries and bring you back into your own land. I will sprinkle clean water on you, and you will be clean; I will cleanse you from all your impurities and from all your idols. I will give you a new heart and put a new spirit in you; I will remove from you your heart of stone and give you a heart of flesh. And I will put my Spirit within you and move you to follow my decrees and be careful to keep my law" (Ezek. 36:24–27 NIV).

2. "But when the kindness and love of God our Savior appeared, he saved us, not because of righteous things we had done, but because of his mercy. He saved us through the washing of rebirth and renewal by the Holy Spirit" (Titus 3:4–5 NIV).

By contrast, "flesh gives birth to flesh," simply means that our carnal bodies are driven by our human desires. Paul painstakingly described his inner conflict in Romans 7:18–20 (NIV): "For I know that good itself does not dwell in me, that is, in my sinful nature. For I have the desire to do what is good, but I cannot carry it out. For I do not do the good I want to do, but the evil I do not want to do—this I keep on doing. Now if I do what I do not want to do, it is no longer I who do it, but it is sin living in me that does it."

REFLECT

1. In John 14:6 (NIV), Jesus said, "I am the way and the truth and the life. No one comes to the Father except through me." Compare this verse to the words, "unless he is born of water and the Spirit," from John 3:5 (above). What do you think Jesus meant when He used the words "except" and "unless?"

2. Review the war of flesh versus spirit that is carefully depicted by Paul. List three ways that you feel the most influence from the flesh. (Include your location, time of day, and who is around you.)

   1)

   2)

   3)

3. List three ways you feel the strongest influence of the Spirit. (Include your location, time of day, and who is around you.)

   1)

   2)

   3)

THE HOLY SPIRIT SANCTIFIES US

But we should always give thanks to God for you, brethren beloved by the Lord, because God has chosen you from the beginning for salvation through sanctification by the Spirit and faith in the truth. (2 Thess. 2:13 NASB)

LEARNING THE SCRIPTURE

1. But we should always give thanks to God for you, brethren beloved by the _____,

2. Because God has chosen you from the beginning for _____ through _____ by the Spirit and faith in the truth.

GOING DEEPER

Paul wrote two letters to the church at Thessolonica following his visit there where he had preached in the synagogue (Acts 17:1–2). He wrote the letters to guide, strengthen, and encourage the young church. In his second letter, he sought to correct some false teaching that had arisen about the second coming of Jesus, provide instructions on how to live a holy life until Christ's return, and comfort them.

In 2 Thessalonians 2:13, Paul assures believers of God's plan for salvation and their security in the plan. "He has saved us and called us to a holy life—not because of anything we have done but because of his own purpose and grace. This grace was given us in Christ Jesus before the beginning of time" (2 Tim. 1:9 NIV).

Sanctification is God's will for us (1 Thess. 4:3). According to Strong's Concordance (38), sanctification is the process of "making or becoming holy" or "being set apart for special use." Sanctification is the work of the Holy Spirit that sets believers on the path to righteousness (Rom. 15:16, 1 Pet. 1:2). This miracle starts at salvation so that the believer is born again and becomes a new creation, leading a life of increasing holiness. "Sanctify them by the truth; your word is truth" (John 17:17 NIV).

REFLECT

1. In 2 Thessalonians 2:13, the words "God," "Lord," and "Spirit" are used. How would you explain the roles of each? Would you conclude that they are three in one? How does this help you in your daily walk with God?

2. Define the word "sanctify."

3. Discuss the sanctifying work of the Spirit.

4. Write a brief summary of when you were saved.

If you are not certain of your salvation, consider discussing this with a pastor or a Christian friend. In Romans 10:9–10 (NIV), Paul writes, "If you declare with your mouth, 'Jesus is Lord,' and believe in your heart that God raised him from the dead, you will be saved. For it is with your heart that you believe and are justified, and it is with your mouth that you profess your faith and are saved." In verse 13 he adds, "Everyone who calls on the name of the Lord will be saved."

If you'd like to receive God's gift of salvation right now, read the prayer below. If you mean this in your heart, then we suggest praying this prayer aloud to accept Christ as your Savior:

> "Dear Lord Jesus, I know I am a sinner, and I ask for Your forgiveness. I believe You died for my sins and rose from the dead. I trust and follow You as my Lord and Savior. Guide my life and help me to do Your will. In Your name, Amen."

Congratulations on your decision! Make sure you're attending a Bible-based church, and surround yourself with other believers to help you start your new life in Jesus.

THE HOLY SPIRIT SEALS US

And you also were included in Christ when you heard the message of truth, the gospel of your salvation. When you believed, you were marked in him with a seal, the promised Holy Spirit, who is a deposit guaranteeing our inheritance until the redemption of those who are God's possession—to the praise of his glory. (Eph. 1:13–14 NIV)

LEARNING THE SCRIPTURE

1. And you also were _____ in Christ when you heard the message of truth, the gospel of your _____.

2. When you believed, you were marked in him with a _____, the promised _____ _____.

3. Who is a deposit _____ our inheritance until the redemption of those who are God's _____—to the praise of his glory.

GOING DEEPER

The Holy Spirit comes to indwell believers when they accept Christ (Rom. 8:9, Acts 2:4, 1 Cor. 6:19 and 12:13), securing and preserving their salvation. The seal of which Paul speaks in his letter to the Ephesians refers to an official mark that was placed on a letter or legal document. The seal signified the ownership, authority, authenticity, and security of the document, and it is used here to indicate that the Holy Spirit "seals" us at salvation—marking us as belonging to God.

The significance of a seal was also extremely important in the stone used to protect the tomb of Christ. Matthew 27:62–66 describes the seal as a security measure used by the Roman leaders. The stone had a seal placed on it to make the tomb secure and prevent the disciples from taking Jesus's body (Matt. 27:64–66) since Jesus promised that He would rise after three days (Matt. 12:40). The importance of a seal is also described in 2 Corinthians 1:21–22 (NIV), "Now it is God who makes both us and you stand firm in Christ. He anointed us, set his seal of ownership on us, and put his Spirit in our hearts as a deposit, guaranteeing what is to come."

REFLECT

1. How do you think the Holy Spirit's seal relates to our salvation? Who is the owner of the seal? Discuss.

2. Read the first two sentences of Ephesians 1:13 above, and compare "when you heard" to "when you believed." How are "hearing" and "believing" related? What happens after believing? Discuss.

3. How is hearing when you're listening to the word of God different from when you listen to something else, such as the news? Explain.

4. Can we lose our seal? Hint: See Romans 8:37. Discuss.

3
THE HOLY SPIRIT

THE HOLY SPIRIT RENEWS US

But when the kindness and love of God our Savior appeared, he saved us, not because of righteous things we had done, but because of his mercy. He saved us through the washing of rebirth and renewal by the Holy Spirit, whom he poured out on us generously through Jesus Christ our Savior, so that, having been justified by his grace, we might become heirs having the hope of eternal life. (Titus 3:4–7 NIV)

LEARNING THE SCRIPTURE

1. But when the kindness and love of God our Savior appeared, he _____ us, not because of _____ _____ we had done, but because of his _____.

2. He saved us through the _____ of _____ and renewal by the Holy Spirit, whom he poured out on us generously through _____ _____ our Savior.

3. So that, having been justified by _____ _____, we might become heirs having the hope of _____ _____.

GOING DEEPER

The book of Titus was written by Paul in about AD 66, as a guide for Titus, a young pastor whom Paul had discipled and left in charge on the island of Crete (Titus 1:5). In this single passage (3:4–7), Paul describes the elements of salvation, each part of which is initiated by and enabled by God and accomplished through the power of the Holy Spirit: His kindness, His love, His mercy, His washing of rebirth and renewal, His son Jesus, and His grace. He offers this salvation, "not because of the righteous things we have done," (Titus 3:5 NIV) but because He "wants all people to be saved and to come to a knowledge of the truth" (1 Tim. 2:4 NIV).

Through the power of the Holy Spirit, which is poured out upon us when we are born again (Rom. 8:9, Acts 2:4, 1 Cor. 6:19 and 12:13), our new life in Christ begins. The Lord "is able to do immeasurably more than all we ask or imagine, according to his power that is at work within us" (Eph. 3:20 NIV). "For it is by grace you have been saved, through faith—and this is not from yourselves, it is the gift of God—not by works, so that no one can boast" (Eph. 2:8–9 NIV).

REFLECT

1. What does renewal mean? When does renewal begin? How long does renewal last? Discuss.

2. Do you think that "washing of rebirth" is related to our spiritual birth? How would you describe the differences among these levels of spiritual maturity:

   1) a spiritual child,

   2) a spiritual adolescent, and

   3) a spiritual adult?

THE HOLY SPIRIT GUARANTEES OUR FUTURE

Now the one who has fashioned us for this very purpose is God, who has given us the Spirit as a deposit, guaranteeing what is to come. (2 Cor. 5:5 NIV)

LEARNING THE SCRIPTURE

1. Now the one who has _____ us for this _____ _____ is God,

2. Who has _____ us the _____ as a deposit, _____ what is to come.

GOING DEEPER

In 2 Corinthians 5:1–11, Paul presents important information to believers about what happens to them after they die: "For we know that if the earthly tent we live in is destroyed, we have a building from God, an eternal house in heaven, not built by human hands" (v. 1 NIV). In verse 5, Paul continues by saying that this was God's plan all along, sending the Holy Spirit to us in the meantime, so there is no doubt about what the future holds. (This is similar to the statement Paul made earlier in 2 Corinthians 1:22 (NIV): "He [God] anointed us, set his seal of ownership on us, and put his Spirit in our hearts as a deposit, guaranteeing what is to come" [clarification added].)

Paul also addressed this in Romans 8, providing the assurance that regardless of circumstances, once we belong to Christ, nothing can change it: "Who shall separate us from the love of Christ? Shall trouble or hardship or persecution or famine or nakedness or danger or sword" (v. 35 NIV). "No, in all these things we are more than conquerors through him who loved us" (v. 37 NIV).

In Philippians, Paul further testifies about our salvation: "In all my prayers for all of you, I always pray with joy because of your partnership in the gospel from the first day until now, being confident of this, that he who began a good work in you will carry it on to completion until the day of Christ Jesus" (Phil. 1:4–6 NIV).

REFLECT

1. We are given the Holy Spirit as the deposit to guarantee what is to come. What does that mean for us? Discuss.

2. Is the Holy Spirit an earnest deposit on a purchase? If so, what is purchased? Explain.

3. In 2 Corinthians 5:5, who do you believe is "guaranteeing" what is to come? Discuss.

4. What is the "very purpose" that Paul mentions in this verse? Discuss.

THE HOLY SPIRIT ASSURES US
THAT CHRIST ABIDES WITH US

The one who keeps His commandments abides in Him, and He in him. We know by this that He abides in us, by the Spirit whom He has given us. (1 John 3:24 NASB)

LEARNING THE SCRIPTURE

1. The one who _____ His [Jesus's] commandments _____ in Him, and He _____ him.

2. We know by this that He _____ in us, by the _____ whom He has given us.

GOING DEEPER

The book of 1 John is believed to have been written by the apostle John, a disciple of Jesus, during the latter part of his life while he was living and preaching in Ephesus. Like Paul (Gal. 1:6–9), John was concerned about the uprising of false teachers and sought to ensure that the churches he was working with were grounded in truth.

This verse is part 1 John 3:19–24, a passage in which John wanted to assure readers of their salvation—and so described the behaviors, which include obeying Christ's commandments, that believers manifest in their lives.

For believers, the blessing promised is that they will abide in Christ, and He in them, which is made possible by the Holy Spirit whom Jesus has sent (John 16:7, 14:16–25).

The evidence of this relationship is the fruit God bears in our lives: "Abide in Me, and I in you. As the branch cannot bear fruit of itself unless it abides in the vine, so neither can you unless you abide in Me. I am the vine, you are the branches; he who abides in Me and I in him, he bears much fruit, for apart from Me you can do nothing" (John 15:4–5 NASB).

REFLECT

1. The word for "abide" in Greek is *menō*, which means "to remain" or "to stay" (Strong's 3306). Are you confident that the Holy Spirit remains in you today? If so, how do you know? If not, see the information about salvation on page 17. Discuss.

2. In 1 John 3:24, John writes that in order to abide with Jesus, we must keep His commandments, which are: "Love the Lord your God with all your heart and with all your soul and with all your mind. This is the first and greatest commandment. And the second is like it: Love your neighbor as yourself" (Matt. 22:37–39 NIV). What does it mean to love your neighbor as yourself? Discuss.

THE HOLY SPIRIT GIVES MEANING TO LIFE

The Spirit gives life; the flesh counts for nothing. The words I have spoken to you—they are full of the Spirit and life. (John 6:63 NIV)

LEARNING THE SCRIPTURE

1. The _____ gives life; the flesh counts for nothing.

2. The words I have _____ to you—they are full of the _____ and _____ .

GOING DEEPER

In this verse, John tells of a time when Jesus was teaching in the synagogue at Capernaum. Jesus was explaining to the disciples that His flesh was true food and His blood was true drink; He defined those who would partake as true followers.

"Just as the living Father sent me and I live because of the Father, so the one who feeds on me will live because of me. This is the bread that came down from heaven. Your ancestors ate manna and died, but whoever feeds on this bread will live forever" (John 6:57–58 NIV).

When the disciples of Jesus heard this, many began to grumble about the teaching being difficult. Jesus may have taken this to mean that their faith was superficial, so He asked, "Does this offend you?" (John 6:61 NIV), or "Does this cause you to stumble?" (John 6:61 NASB).

The word "stumble" translates to a form of the Greek verb *skandalizo*. This can either mean "to take offense" or "to fall into a trap" (Strong's 4624). Jesus continues the dialogue with many that grumbled by inquiring, "What if you see the Son of Man ascend to where he was before!" (John 6:62 NIV). Later many of His disciples turned back and no longer followed Him. He then asked of the twelve disciples, "You do not want to leave too, do you?" (John 6:67 NIV). Peter answered by saying that only Jesus had the words of eternal life (v. 6:68).

REFLECT

1. Christ presented the inverse relationship between the Holy Spirit and flesh. Do you think He anticipated the reaction He got from the crowd? Do you think that He was testing His followers for a reason? Explain.

2. Jesus asked the disciples if His teaching was difficult and caused them to "stumble." What things in your life cause you to stumble? Discuss.

3. When you stumble, what can you do to get back on track? Discuss.

4
THE HOLY SPIRIT

THE HOLY SPIRIT LIVES IN US

But you know him, for he lives with you and will be in you. (John 14:17 NIV)

And in him you too are being built together to become a dwelling in which God lives by his Spirit. (Eph. 2:22 NIV)

LEARNING THE SCRIPTURE

1. But you know him, for he lives _____ you and will be _____ you.

2. And in him you too are being built together to become a _____ in which God lives by his _____.

GOING DEEPER

On the night of the Last Supper, Jesus told the disciples that He would ask the Father to send an advocate, the Holy Spirit, to be with them forever (John 14:16). An important aspect of that promise was that the Holy Spirit would not only be *with* them but would also *live in* them.

Likewise, in Ephesians, Paul tells us that believers will be indwelled by the Holy Spirit. He says in Ephesians 2:19–21 (NIV), "Consequently, you are no longer foreigners and strangers, but fellow citizens with God's people and also members of his household,

 built on the foundation of the apostles and prophets, with Christ Jesus himself as the chief cornerstone. In him the whole building is joined together and rises to become a holy temple in the Lord."

The most important aspect of any building is the foundation itself, where we find Christ as the chief cornerstone. The cornerstone was a key structural support to ancient buildings. It was precisely positioned because of the interdependence of all structural parts of the building. It was the support, the orienting element, and the unifier of the entire structure.

This is what Jesus Christ is to God's kingdom, God's family, and God's church. The dwelling itself (our bodies) is the place in which God lives (inhabits) by His Holy Spirit.

"Do you not know that your bodies are temples of the Holy Spirit, who is in you, whom you have received from God?" (1 Cor. 6:19 NIV). The Holy Spirit lives in the spiritual body of the redeemed.

REFLECT

1. What is your definition of a temple? Explain.

2. Since your body is a temple of the Holy Spirit, are there ways that you sense His presence? Discuss.

3. In Ephesians 2:22, Paul says that "you too are being built together to become a dwelling." Does this mean that we are a work in progress?

4. List a few ways that you could improve your temple.

THE HOLY SPIRIT FILLS US

Do not get drunk on wine, which leads to debauchery. Instead, be filled with the Spirit, speaking to one another with psalms, hymns, and songs from the Spirit. Sing and make music from your heart to the Lord, always giving thanks to God the Father for everything, in the name of our Lord Jesus Christ. (Eph. 5:18–20 NIV)

LEARNING THE SCRIPTURE

1. Do not get drunk on _____, which leads to debauchery. Instead be filled with the _____, speaking to one another with _____, _____ and songs from _____ _____.

2. Sing and make music _____ _____ _____ to the Lord, always giving thanks to God the Father _____ _____, in the name of our Lord Jesus Christ.

GOING DEEPER

Although drunkenness is consistently condemned throughout the Bible (Prov. 21:1, Gal. 5:21, 1 Pet. 5:8, 1 Cor. 6:10), in this instance Paul may be comparing the alcoholic intoxication that was part of pagan religious rituals of the day with true communion with God through the filling of the Holy Spirit—which produces lasting joy. Jesus promised this filling in the Sermon on the Mount, "Blessed are those who hunger and thirst for righteousness, for they will be filled" (Matt. 5:6 NIV).

In Greek, the word for "fill" is *plērousthe,* meaning "to make full," "to fill to individual capacity," or "to complete" (Strong's 4137). This starts by focusing on Christ: "Let the message of Christ dwell among you richly as you teach and admonish one another with all wisdom through psalms, hymns, and songs from the Spirit, singing to God with gratitude in your hearts. And whatever you do, whether in word or deed, do it all in the name of the Lord Jesus, giving thanks to God the Father through him" (Col. 3:16–17 NIV).

The goal is to keep ourselves constantly filled as we yield to the continual leading of the Holy Spirit. Being filled with the Spirit is consciously living under the influence of Jesus

Christ and letting God's Word guide us through everything we think and do; it is allowing the Holy Spirit to "complete" us.

REFLECT

1. In Ephesians 5:18–20, we see the contrast between being drunk with wine and being filled with the Spirit. List some of the qualities that a person might exhibit who has been "filled with the Spirit."

2. Are there times when you sing hymns or praise music and feel joy? Is there a difference between singing hymns or praise music and singing popular songs? Discuss.

3. How might the Holy Spirit use your joy to help others who may be alone, hospitalized, or in a nursing home? Discuss.

THE HOLY SPIRIT EMPOWERS US

*I am going to send you what my Father has promised; but stay in the city
until you have been clothed with power from on high.* (Luke 24:49 NIV)

LEARNING THE SCRIPTURE

1. I am going to send you what my Father has _____.

2. Stay in the city until you have been _____ with _____ from on high.

GOING DEEPER

The gospel of Luke and its sequel, Acts, span more than sixty years and provide details about John the Baptist; the birth, life, death, resurrection, and ascension of Jesus; the coming of the Holy Spirit; the history of the early Christian church; and the actions of the apostles. Luke also contains genealogy, sermons, and parables.

In his gospel, Luke's goal was to "compile an account of the things accomplished among us, just as they were handed down to us by those who from the beginning were eyewitnesses and servants of the word, it seemed fitting for me as well, having investigated everything carefully from the beginning, to write it out for you in consecutive order" (Luke 1:1–3 NASB).

In Luke 24:49, the author records Jesus's instructions to the disciples during a time that was after His resurrection and shortly before His ascension. In fact, this verse contains the final recorded words of Jesus before He ascended into heaven. Jesus told the disciples to wait in Jerusalem for "what my Father has promised," the coming of the Holy Spirit, which happened ten days later at Pentecost. Had the disciples left and gone to their own homes, the start of the Christian church may have fizzled out—not having the united impact of the Holy Spirit upon the world.

In Acts 1:8 (NIV), Luke also wrote about the empowerment we receive from the Holy Spirit: "But you will receive power when the Holy Spirit comes on you; and you will be my witnesses in Jerusalem, and in all Judea and Samaria, and to the ends of the earth." We are to be Christ's witnesses, sharing the good news in our cities, in our states and countries, and anywhere else God sends us.

REFLECT

1. Define resurrection and ascension. Which happened first? Explain.

2. What does it mean to be "clothed" with power from on high? Discuss.

3. How could the Holy Spirit empower you to help to others?

THE HOLY SPIRIT EMBOLDENS US

After they prayed, the place where they were meeting was shaken. And they were all filled with the Holy Spirit and spoke the word of God boldly.
(Acts 4:31 NIV)

LEARNING THE SCRIPTURE

1. After they prayed, the place where they were meeting was _____.

2. They were _____ filled with the Holy Spirit and spoke the word of God _____.

GOING DEEPER

In this verse, Luke describes an event that happened after the resurrection of Jesus. The Sanhedrin, the ruling Jewish council in Jerusalem, arrested Peter and John, who had healed a lame beggar (Acts 3:1–10) and were speaking and preaching about the miraculous powers of Jesus. The rulers asked them: "By what power or what name did you do this?" (Acts 4:7 NIV).

Peter, filled with the Holy Spirit, told them the healing had happened by the name of Jesus Christ (Acts 4:8). "When they saw the courage of Peter and John and realized that they were unschooled, ordinary men, they were astonished and they took note that these men had been with Jesus" (v. 13 NIV). The rulers could see that the lame man had been healed, so they released Peter and John but warned them not to teach in Jesus's name again (v. 18).

Peter and John asked the Lord to "consider their threats [those of the Sanhedrin] and enable your servants to speak your word with great boldness" (Acts 4:29 NIV, clarification added). Then it happened! As on Pentecost, a physical phenomenon signaled the presence of the Holy Spirit. Peter and John and all of the people who were gathered there were filled with the Holy Spirit, and they spoke the word of God with boldness and without fear, not only among themselves, but publicly.

REFLECT

1. "Embolden" is defined by www.merriam-webster.com as "to instill with boldness or courage." Has there been a time when you felt emboldened to testify about an experience or special moment with God? Discuss.

2. Is it possible you were being influenced by the Holy Spirit? Explain how that made you feel. How did the person or people you were speaking to respond?

5
THE HOLY SPIRIT

THE HOLY SPIRIT ENABLES US TO WORSHIP

God is spirit, and his worshipers must worship in the Spirit and in truth.
(John 4:24 NIV)

LEARNING THE SCRIPTURE

1. God is _____.

2. And his worshipers must worship in the _____ and in _____.

GOING DEEPER

This verse comes from a conversation between Jesus and a Samaritan woman at a well. Jesus and His disciples were traveling from Judea to Galilee, taking a route that took them through Samaria. The purpose of going through this town was so that Jesus could meet a certain woman, a meeting that was planned before the world existed.

This beautiful story of God's love puts Jesus alone with the woman, as the disciples had gone into town to get something to eat. It was around noon and Jesus stopped by the well to get a drink of water. Interestingly, He had come to Jacob's well (John 4:1–6), which is fed by a spring of fresh water (streams of living waters) about 100 feet below.

A Samaritan woman was coming to the well for water, but she did not realize who awaited her. Perhaps the woman had come to this well—at least half a mile from where she lived—and at this time of day to avoid seeing anyone else, because of her shame of having had several husbands (John 4:18). There were other wells closer to her home, and women usually drew water early in the day or late in the afternoon to avoid the midday heat.

When the woman arrived, Jesus asked her for a drink. Since Jesus was a Jew and the woman was a Samaritan, it was improper for her to get Him a drink (John 4:9). In this encounter, Jesus revealed to her that He, in fact, was the "living water" saying, "Woman, believe me, a time is coming when you will worship the Father neither on this mountain nor in Jerusalem. You Samaritans worship what you do not know; we worship what we do know, for salvation is from the Jews. Yet a time is coming and has now come when the true worshipers will worship the Father in the Spirit and in truth, for they are the kind of worshipers the Father seeks. God is spirit, and his worshipers must worship in the Spirit and in truth."

The woman said, "I know that Messiah" (called Christ) "is coming. When he comes, he will explain everything to us." Then Jesus declared, "I, the one speaking to you—I am he" (vv. 21–26 NIV).

REFLECT

1. Who did the woman encounter at the well? Who did she think the man was?

2. If she was trying to avoid being confronted because of her sins, how did Christ respond in verse 4:18? What did Jesus reveal when the woman testified of the coming Messiah?

3. What is significant about Christ sitting above a spring-fed well compared to the springs of living waters? Hint: See John 7:38.

4. The woman at the well may have been avoiding people by choosing to draw water at a well that was a half mile away from town. Have you avoided people in your life because you simply felt "beneath" them or uncomfortable being around them? How did the Holy Spirit help you in that situation?

THE HOLY SPIRIT HELPS US PRAY

And pray in the Spirit on all occasions with all kinds of prayers and requests. With this in mind, be alert and always keep on praying for all the Lord's people. (Eph. 6:18 NIV)

LEARNING THE SCRIPTURE

1. Pray in the Spirit on _____ _____ with _____ _____ of prayers and requests.

2. Be _____ and always keep on praying for all the _____ _____.

GOING DEEPER

To pray in the Spirit is to pray in the name of Christ and in accordance to His will, and in union with the Holy Spirit, who helps us in our weakness (Rom 8:26). As to the importance of prayer, Paul says we are told to pray on all occasions, with all kinds of prayers, to always keep praying for all of God's people. This is so we are mindful that in ALL things we should rely on God. In Acts 18:1, Jesus told the disciples that they should always pray and not give up.

This does not mean to pray in a formal or ritualistic way at all times, but rather to be in a continual awareness of, and dependence on, God. In Colossians 4:2 (NIV), Paul instructs us to "devote yourselves to prayer, being watchful and thankful." In Greek, the verb for "devote" is *proskartereō*, meaning "to continue" or "to persevere" (Strong's 4342).

Scripture indicates that it is appropriate to pray at any time, in any location, and in any situation. "Do not be anxious about anything, but in every situation, by prayer and petition, with thanksgiving, present your requests to God. And the peace of God, which transcends all understanding, will guard your hearts and your minds in Christ Jesus" (Phil. 4:6–7 NIV).

As believers, one of the best things we can do is to pray for each other. As part of the Body of Christ, when one member is weak or struggling, the other members help support and strengthen that person. "Therefore confess your sins to each other and pray for each other so that you may be healed. The prayer of a righteous person is powerful and effective" (James 5:16 NIV).

REFLECT

1. What three words describe your prayer life?

    1)

    2)

    3)

2. Do you have a special time or place set aside for conversations with God? Why or why not? Discuss.

3. We are told to pray in the Spirit on all occasions, with all kinds of prayers. Name five things to pray about.

    1)

    2)

    3)

    4)

    5)

Not sure what to pray about? You can always pray the prayer Jesus taught His disciples, the Lord's Prayer: "Our Father in heaven, hallowed be your name, your kingdom come, your will be done, on earth as it is in heaven. Give us today our daily bread. And forgive us our debts, as we also have forgiven our debtors. And lead us not into temptation, but deliver us from the evil one" (Matt. 6:9–13 NIV).

THE HOLY SPIRIT INTERCEDES FOR US

In the same way the Spirit also helps our weakness; for we do not know how to pray as we should, but the Spirit Himself intercedes for us with groanings too deep for words; and He who searches the hearts knows what the mind of the Spirit is, because He intercedes for the saints according to the will of God. (Rom. 8:26–27 NASB)

LEARNING THE SCRIPTURE

1. In the same way the Spirit also _____ our _____;

2. For we do not know _____ _____ _____ as we should, but the Spirit Himself _____ for us with _____ too deep for words;

3. And he who _____ _____ _____ knows what the mind of the Spirit is, because He intercedes for the _____ according to the _____ _____ _____.

GOING DEEPER

We do not have to go through life alone—the Holy Spirit is here to help us. The Greek word for "help," *sunantilambanomai*, means "to take hold with," "to lend a hand with," or "to supply assistance that exactly corresponds to the need" (Strong's 4878). In other words, the Holy Spirit is in this life with us.

Because of our susceptibility to sin and doubt, the Holy Spirit helps us in our weakness, whether it is from our general humanity or a specific weakness. Even after salvation, we are subject to spiritual weaknesses. Conversely, doing good things is a result of the Spirit working in and through us.

Paul goes on to say that we do not pray as we should and that the Spirit prays on our behalf. Even the most faithful Christians cannot know all of God's will for our lives or for the lives of those for whom we are praying. Paul says that assistance comes from the Spirit Himself, interceding for us in ways that are beyond human comprehension but that are understood by God.

REFLECT

1. Who are the saints in Romans 8:27? Explain.

2. How does the Holy Spirit intercede for the saints? Discuss.

3. Does it help to know that the Holy Spirit refines our prayers when He takes them to God? Explain.

THE HOLY SPIRIT PROVIDES ACCESS TO THE FATHER

He came and preached peace to you who were far away and peace to those who were near. For through him we both have access to the Father by one Spirit. (Eph. 2:17—18 NIV)

LEARNING THE SCRIPTURE

1. He (Jesus Christ) came and _____ _____ to you who were far away and peace to those who were near.

2. For through _____ we both have access to the _____ by one _____.

GOING DEEPER

In Paul's letter to the Ephesians, he wanted to remind them of the things he had taught them during his three-year stay in Ephesus (Acts 20:31). In Ephesians 2:13–18, Paul emphasized unity in the body of Christ and the importance of peace.

Those who were "far away" were the Gentiles who had come to Christ. Jewish converts considered themselves to be "near." But in Christ, all believers are brought close to God.

When we receive Christ, we are granted access to God through faith in Christ's sacrifice on the cross (Eph. 3:12, Rom. 5:2). The Greek word for "access" is *prosagógé*, which implies the concept of not having access on our own merit but being granted the right to come before God—knowing we will be welcomed (Strong's 4318). The resources of the Trinity belong to the faithful, and the Holy Spirit presents believers before the heavenly throne of God the Father, where they are welcome to come with boldness at any time (Rom. 8:15–17, Gal. 4:6–7, Heb. 4:16).

In Romans 8:17 (NIV) Paul declares, "Now if we are children, we are heirs—heirs of God and co-heirs with Christ, if indeed we share in his sufferings in order that we may also share in his glory."

REFLECT

1. What do you think it means to have access to the Father by the Holy Spirit? Discuss.

2. Read Romans 8:15–17. How is the Trinity of God referenced in this passage? Discuss.

6
THE HOLY SPIRIT

51

THE HOLY SPIRIT TEACHES US ABOUT THE FORGIVENESS OF SIN

For by one sacrifice he has made perfect forever those who are being made holy. The Holy Spirit also testifies to us about this. First he says: "This is the covenant I will make with them after that time, says the Lord. I will put my laws in their hearts, and I will write them on their minds."

Then he adds: "Their sins and lawless acts I will remember no more." And where these have been forgiven, sacrifice for sin is no longer necessary. (Heb. 10:14–18 NIV)

LEARNING THE SCRIPTURE

1. For by one _____ he has made _____ _____ those who are being made holy. The Holy Spirit also _____ to us about this.

2. First he says: "This is the _____ I will make with them after that time, says the Lord. I will put my _____ in their _____, and I will write them on their minds."

3. Then he adds: "Their _____ and lawless acts I will _____ _____ _____." And where these have been _____, sacrifice for sin is ____ _____ _____.

GOING DEEPER

The overall theme of the book of Hebrews is to present Jesus Christ as perfect and superior to everyone and to anything Judaism and the old covenant had to offer. The author is unknown; the audience was a mix of Jewish believers and non-believers. Early

Jewish Christians were under intense persecution and some were contemplating a return to Judaism. The writer encouraged them not to turn away from Christ as their only hope of salvation.

In this passage, we learn more about the completeness of salvation. The "sacrifice" mentioned in verse 14 refers to the death of Jesus Christ, who removes sin forever in those who belong to Him. This does not mean that we are no longer aware of our sin, but that we have been permanently and eternally forgiven, and therefore are delivered from the fear of judgement. This also does not mean that we should willfully ignore the way that God wants us to live. Quite the opposite is true. As members of Christ's earthly body, we strive to live a holy life (Rom. 12:2, 1 Pet. 1:13–25, Ps. 51:10, 2 Cor. 7:1, Prov. 28:13, John 15:3, Rom. 6:14).

We often think of the word "covenant" as a contract or agreement. But the original Greek word, *diathēkē*, corresponds more closely to our present-day "last will and testament" (Strong's 1242). A will does not take effect until the person making the will dies. This helps us understand why the "New Covenant" did not go into effect until after the death of Christ.

With our salvation secure and our sins forgiven, the Holy Spirit teaches us directly about God's laws and puts an understanding about them in our hearts and minds. As 2 Corinthians 3:3 (NIV) tells us, "You show that you are a letter from Christ, the result of our ministry, written not with ink but with the Spirit of the living God, not on tablets of stone but on tablets of human hearts."

Finally, and to our great joy, our sins are not only forgiven, they are forgotten. The work of Christ's sacrifice is done, final, complete, and unchangeable.

REFLECT

1. Read Jeremiah 31:33–34. How do these verses relate to Hebrews 10:14–18? Discuss.

2. What does Hebrews 10:17–18 say about sin? Discuss.

3. List three ways that knowing your sins are forgiven helps you in your daily walk with God.

   1)

   2)

   3)

THE HOLY SPIRIT FREES US FROM SIN AND DEATH

Therefore there is now no condemnation for those who are in Christ Jesus. For the law of the Spirit of life in Christ Jesus has set you free from the law of sin and death. (Rom. 8:1–2 NASB)

LEARNING THE SCRIPTURE

1. Therefore there is now _____ _____ for those who are in Christ Jesus.

2. For the law of the Spirit of life in Christ Jesus has _____ _____ _____

from the law of sin and death.

GOING DEEPER:

Romans 8:1–2 is filled with hope for a hurting world. In it, Paul tells us that for believers, "the law of sin and death" is made "null and void." Because Jesus has paid the penalty for all of our sins, we have been set free. We didn't earn this freedom; it was given to us through the amazing sacrifice made by Jesus. Christ fulfilled the old law and gave us a new, simple law that produces life: the law that requires faith (Rom. 3:27).

Release from the law's condemnation does not mean release from the law's requirements and standards. The freedom that Christ gives from sin's power also gives believers the ability—and desire—to obey God. This is made possible by the indwelling power and direction of the Holy Spirit in the believer's life (Rom. 8:6–7).

"Before the coming of this faith, we were held in custody under the law, locked up until the faith that was to come would be revealed. So the law was our guardian until Christ came that we might be justified by faith. Now that this faith has come, we are no longer under a guardian" (Gal. 3:23–25 NIV).

REFLECT

1. How does the law compare with the grace given by Jesus? Discuss.

2. Is it possible to "earn" salvation? Discuss.

3. What's been your greatest challenge since becoming a Christian? Discuss.

THE HOLY SPIRIT GUIDES US AWAY FROM SIN

So I say, walk by the Spirit, and you will not gratify the desires of the flesh. (Gal. 5:16 NIV)

LEARNING THE SCRIPTURE

1. So I say, walk by the _____,

2. And you will not gratify the _____ of the _____.

GOING DEEPER

In Galatians, Paul repeatedly stresses the contrast between the law and grace. A person cannot achieve salvation or sustain living in God through keeping the law. In order for us to live a holy life in accordance to the will of God, we need the Holy Spirit, who is given to us the moment we believe (Rom. 8:9, Acts 2:4, 1 Cor. 6:19 and 12:13). The Spirit is a permanent, indwelling guide who teaches (2 Tim. 1:13–14) and strengthens us (Luke 24:49, 1 Cor. 12:6).

The phrase "walk by the Spirit" in the present tense indicates that Paul is speaking of a continuous, ongoing action. Walking brings progress, going from where we are to where we are supposed to go. Step-by-step (glory to glory [2 Cor. 3:18 KJV]), the Spirit moves us toward God and where He wants us to be.

While it is the Spirit who is the source and power of holy living, it is the believer who is commanded to walk. The believer who is led by the Spirit must be willing to go where the Spirit guides and to do what the Spirit leads him or her to do.

To "walk by the Spirit" means we obey God, to our own benefit: "As for everyone who comes to me and hears my words and puts them into practice, I will show you what they are like. They are like a man building a house, who dug down deep and laid the foundation on rock. When a flood came, the torrent struck that house but could not shake it, because it was well built. But the one who hears my words and does not put them into practice is like a man who built a house on the ground without a foundation. The moment the torrent struck that house, it collapsed and its destruction was complete" (Luke 6:47–49 NIV).

REFLECT

1. Does Galatians 5:16 suggest that Spirit and flesh are at odds with each other? Why or why not? Explain.

2. Since we are encouraged by Paul to "walk by the Spirit," what is our ultimate destination?

3. How does gratification of the flesh get in your way of walking with the Holy Spirit? Make a list.

THE HOLY SPIRIT TEACHES US ABOUT GOD

I keep asking that the God of our Lord Jesus Christ, the glorious Father, may give you the Spirit of wisdom and revelation, so that you may know him better. (Eph. 1:17 NIV)

LEARNING THE SCRIPTURE

1. I keep asking that the _____ of our Lord _____ _____, the glorious Father,

2. May give you the _____ of wisdom and revelation, so that _____ may know _____ better.

GOING DEEPER

In his letter to the Ephesians, Paul prays that God will help us recognize "whose" we are in Christ rather than "who" we are. We sometimes fail to appreciate the unlimited blessings that belong to those with a relationship in Christ. Paul's request is directed to the Father who imparts the Holy Spirit for the purpose of illuminating how unlimited our blessings are just to know Christ better (John 14:25–26).

Likewise, James, the half-brother of Jesus, tells us the source of wisdom is God: "If any of you lacks wisdom, you should ask God, who gives generously to all without finding fault, and it will be given to you" (James 1:5 NIV). And that godly wisdom comes from above: "But the wisdom that comes from heaven is first of all pure; then peace-loving, considerate, submissive, full of mercy and good fruit, impartial and sincere" (James 3:17 NIV).

Believers often search for an extra "something" that ordinary life lacks. Peter gives us the answer: "His divine power has given us everything we need for a godly life through our knowledge of him who called us by his own glory and goodness" (2 Pet. 1:3 NIV).

REFLECT

1. In Ephesians 1:17, who is the Spirit of wisdom? Explain.

2. If we lack wisdom, what does James suggest we do in verse 1:5? Discuss.

3. James says that God gives generously without finding fault (James 1:5). What could this convey to people who are without hope, are imprisoned, or are spiritually lost? Discuss.

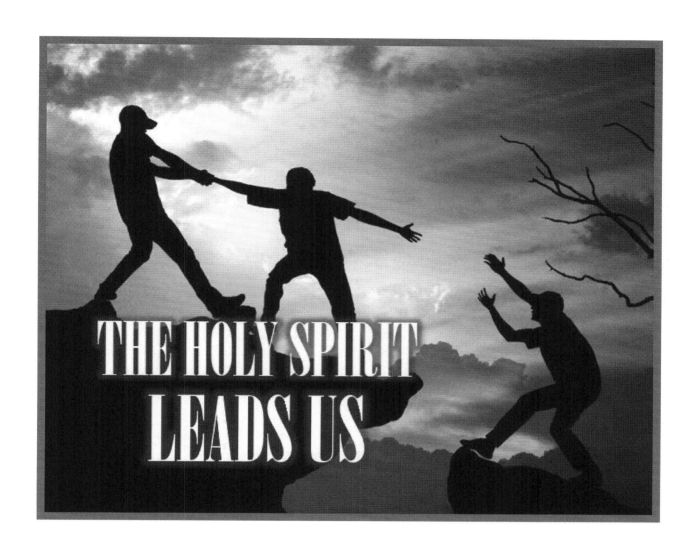

7
THE HOLY SPIRIT

THE HOLY SPIRIT LEADS US

But if you are led by the Spirit, you are not under the law. (Gal. 5:18 NIV)

LEARNING THE SCRIPTURE

1. But if you are led by the _____, you are not under the _____.

GOING DEEPER

"For those who are led by the Spirit of God are the children of God" (Rom. 8:14 NIV). "So I say walk by the Spirit, and you will not gratify the desires of the flesh" (Gal. 5:16 NIV). Being led by the Spirit is the true path of freedom, as opposed to following the law of Moses. In Galatians, Paul tells us that the law will not save or sanctify us. However, if we are guided by the Holy Spirit, who is given to us at our salvation (Rom. 8:9, Acts 2:4, 1 Cor. 6:19 and 12:13), the condemnation of the old law does not apply.

But how do we follow the guidance of the Holy Spirit? Discerning God's will can be one of the most challenging things that Christian's face. Some ways God leads us include:

- Through scripture: Sometimes the Holy Spirit helps us understand a passage in a new way that gives us insight into a situation (John 16:13).
- Through life circumstances: God may open or close a door that can lead us in a different direction (Rev. 3:8).
- Through the counsel of other believers: Proverbs 11:14 and 15:22 indicate that it is helpful to get advice from others when making important decisions.

Even so, there may be times when you just don't "feel" led. John tells us that Jesus said, "If you love me, keep my commands" (John 14:15 NIV). So even if we don't seem to have direct guidance, if we love God, we will not do anything we understand to be wrong.

But for many of us, we often don't recognize that we were being led except in hindsight. In a booklet entitled *Guidance*, author Philip Yancey wrote:

> I have a confession to make. For me, at least, guidance only becomes evident when I look backward, months and years later. Then the circuitous process falls into place and the hand of God seems clear. But at that moment of decision, I feel mainly confusion and uncertainty. Indeed, almost all the guidance in my life has been subtle and indirect.
>
> This pattern has recurred so often (and clear guidance for the future has occurred so seldom), that I am about to conclude that we have a basic direction wrong. I had always

thought of guidance as forward-looking. We keep praying, hoping, counting on God to reveal what we should do next. In my own experience, at least, I have found the direction to be reversed. The focus must be on the moment before me, the present. How is my relationship to God? As circumstances change, for better or worse, will I respond with obedience and trust?

REFLECT

1. Are there ways that you recognize the Spirit's leading? Explain.

2. When do you notice it the most? When do you notice it the least? Discuss.

3. Can you list three ways the Holy Spirit could lead you more easily?

   1)

   2)

   3)

THE HOLY SPIRIT SPEAKS TO US

Whoever has ears, let them hear what the Spirit says to the churches. To the one who is victorious, I will give the right to eat from the tree of life, which is in the paradise of God. (Rev. 2:7 NIV)

LEARNING THE SCRIPTURE

1. Whoever has _____, let them _____ what the Spirit says to the churches.

2. To the one who is victorious, I will give the right to _____ _____ _____ _____

   _____ _____, which is in the _____ of God.

GOING DEEPER

The book of Revelation was written by the apostle John during the latter part of his life. He also wrote the gospel and the three epistles (letters) that bear his name. Revelation predicts the second coming of Jesus Christ and the restoration of the earth.

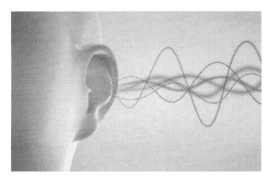

In Revelation, John sends letters to seven churches in Asia Minor (primarily in what is present-day Turkey) instructing those who have ears to listen to what the Spirit says. Each of the letters is different, but the final paragraph in all of them includes the directive to listen to the Spirit. While the letters were written to churches at the time, the message about listening is relevant for us today.

Some suggestions for listening include:

- Spend time in the Bible. Through studying Scripture, we have the opportunity for God to reveal new levels of understanding and discernment about what is written.

- Consider identifying a place and time to meet with God every day. Scripture gives us a model for listening to God, "Let the morning bring me word of your unfailing love, for I have put my trust in you. Show me the way I should go, for to you I entrust my life" (Ps. 143:8 NIV).

- Find a peaceful time and space to focus on God. If you want to hear His message it is helpful to be still and quiet your mind, gently pushing away intruding thoughts. "Be still, and know that I am God" (Ps. 46:10 NIV).

- Talk to God through prayer. Think of prayer as a conversation with God—it doesn't have to be formal. Regular conversations with God can transform your life.

- Have a receptive attitude. Remember that we don't have all the answers and need God's help.

- Thank God for helping you. As we recognize and appreciate how God is working in our lives, we will be aware of it more often.

REFLECT

1. How have you been listening for the Holy Spirit? Are there things that happen to help you recognize when He is speaking to you? Explain.

2. Are there ways that you could be more receptive to what the Holy Spirit is saying to you?

3. List two ways you can find more time to listen for the Holy Spirit.

THE HOLY SPIRIT HELPS US
REMEMBER GOD'S TEACHING

What you heard from me, keep as the pattern of sound teaching, with faith and love in Christ Jesus. Guard the good deposit that was entrusted to you—guard it with the help of the Holy Spirit who lives in us. (2 Tim. 1:13–14 NIV)

LEARNING THE SCRIPTURE

1. What you heard from me, keep as the _____ of sound _____, with faith and love in _____ _____.

2. Guard the _____ _____ that was _____ to you,

3. Guard it with the help of the _____ _____ who _____ _____ us.

GOING DEEPER

Second Timothy is Paul's last communication, written while he was in a Roman prison (2 Tim. 2:9), and knowing that his life was nearly over (2 Tim. 4:6). In this letter, which is sometimes referred to as Paul's "Last Will and Testament," he relays information that he feels is important for Timothy in order to protect and grow the Christian church. Timothy was the leader of the church in Ephesus (1 Tim. 1:3), where Paul had preached for three years (Acts 20:31).

Paul tells Timothy to hold fast to the sound doctrine with which he has been entrusted and that the Holy Spirit will help him faithfully share the information with others.

Paul adds instructions that are especially relevant today: "I give you this charge: Preach the word; be prepared in season and out of season; correct, rebuke and encourage—with great patience and careful instruction. For the time will come when people will not put up with sound doctrine. Instead, to suit their own desires, they will gather around them a great number of teachers to say what their itching ears want to hear. They will turn their ears away from the truth and turn aside to myths. But you, keep your head in all situations, endure hardship, do the work of an evangelist, discharge all the duties of your ministry" (2 Tim. 4:1–5 NIV).

REFLECT

1. What is the "good deposit?" To whom was it entrusted? Discuss.

2. How does the Holy Spirit guard the good deposit made in us to mature our faith? Discuss.

3. If you were leaving final advice to someone about the most important things in life, what would you say? Write down what you would tell that person.

THE HOLY SPIRIT SHOWS US
WHAT IS PLEASING TO GOD

For the kingdom of God is not a matter of eating and drinking, but of righteousness, peace and joy in the Holy Spirit, because anyone who serves Christ in this way is pleasing to God and receives human approval. (Rom. 14:17–18 NIV)

LEARNING THE SCRIPTURE

1. For the _____ of God is not a matter of _____ and _____, but of

   righteousness, _____ and _____ in the Holy Spirit,

2. Because anyone who serves _____ in this way is _____ to_____

   and receives _____ approval.

GOING DEEPER

In Paul's letter to the church in Rome, he described some of the practical aspects of living in a way that is pleasing to God. Because the first converts to Christianity were coming from the Jewish faith or were Gentiles, one of the topics Paul covered was how to live in fellowship and unity with other Christians.

In Romans 14:17–18, Paul proactively addressed the laws about which foods could be eaten and when, and how the food was to be prepared. Since early Christians were from different beliefs—and had different requirements for food—the subject was bound to come up. Paul did not want people to argue about food and explained that it was more important to treat each other with kindness and respect, building each other up. The qualities of righteousness, peace, and joy are pleasing to God, and when they are manifested in believers, the work of Christ is advanced.

REFLECT

1. Read 1 Corinthians 9:12, Romans 12:10, and Romans 14:21. What is the recurring theme about our treatment of fellow Christians?

2. The qualities of "righteousness, peace, and joy," are said to be pleasing to God. List three other qualities that are pleasing to God.

   1)

   2)

   3)

8
THE HOLY SPIRIT

THE HOLY SPIRIT PROTECTS US

Take the helmet of salvation and the sword of the Spirit, which is the word of God. (Eph. 6:17 NIV)

When the enemy shall come in like a flood, the Spirit of the LORD shall lift up a standard against him. (Isa. 59:19 KJV)

LEARNING THE SCRIPTURE

1. Take the _____ of _____, and the _____ _____ _____ _____ which is the _____ of God.

2. When the _____ shall come in _____ ____ _____, the Spirit of the LORD shall lift up a _____ against him.

GOING DEEPER

In Ephesians, Paul uses the imagery of a Roman soldier to depict the spiritual defenses at our disposal in order to do battle with the adversary. Ephesians 6:17 is part of a longer passage about "the armor of God":

"Therefore put on the full armor of God, so that when the day of evil comes, you may be able to stand your ground, and after you have done everything, to stand. Stand firm then, with the **belt of truth** buckled around your waist, with the **breastplate of righteousness** in place, and with your feet fitted with the readiness that comes from the **gospel of peace**. In addition to all this, take up the **shield of faith**, with which you can extinguish all the flaming arrows of the evil one. Take the **helmet of salvation** and the **sword of the Spirit**, which is the word of God" (Eph. 6:13–17 NIV, emphasis added).

Throughout his writings, Paul describes the struggle between the flesh and the spirit, and warfare with the enemy. Because Christians belong to God, they may be drawn into this spiritual conflict and attacked by the enemy. This is the same enemy that was made known in Eden (Gen. 3) and continues through this time. We may find ourselves on the battleground but can protect ourselves with the armor God provides.

REFLECT

1. Has there been a time when you felt like you were under a spiritual attack? What was it, and how did you handle it? Can someone else learn from or benefit from your experience? Discuss.

2. Are there situations or circumstances in which you feel pressured or tempted to do something you know is not right? Does knowing that you have the armor of God available help you resist temptation? Discuss.

3. Why is it helpful to be girded in the word of God? Explain.

THE HOLY SPIRIT TESTIFIES THAT
WE ARE CHILDREN OF GOD

The Spirit himself testifies with our spirit that we are God's children.
(Rom. 8:16 NIV)

LEARNING THE SCRIPTURE

1. The _____ himself testifies with our spirit that we are God's _____.

GOING DEEPER

In ancient Rome, adoption of boys was fairly common particularly in the upper political class. The need for a male heir was a strong incentive to have at least one son. Adoption also cemented family ties, fostering and reinforcing alliances. Upon the father's death, the adopted son would sometimes inherit the father's title, bulk of the estate, and obligation to carry on the family name.

Because of its importance, the adoption process involved several legal steps including the presence of seven reputable witnesses who could testify, if needed, to any challenge of the adoption after the father's death.

Paul would likely have been familiar with this process and may have had it in mind when he wrote this part of Romans. He assures us the Holy Spirit Himself is our witness that we have been adopted by God. As God's children, we can have an intimate and dependent relationship with Him, free from the fear of condemnation.

John also provides this assurance: "Yet to all who did receive him, to those who believed in his name, he gave the right to become children of God—children born not of natural descent, nor of human decision or a husband's will, but born of God" (John 1:12–13 NIV).

REFLECT

1. In John 1:12, what is required to be a child of God? Describe.

2. Read Luke 20:36. What does it mean to be "children of the resurrection?" Explain.

3. As a child of God, is there anything you've avoided saying to your heavenly Father? How would it help you if you were to speak to God about what is on your heart? Reflect and discuss.

THE HOLY SPIRIT REVEALS GOD'S THOUGHTS TO US

For who knows a person's thoughts except their own spirit within them? In the same way no one knows the thoughts of God except the Spirit of God. (1 Cor. 2:11 NIV)

LEARNING THE SCRIPTURE

1. For who knows a person's thought except their own _____ within them?

2. In the same way no one knows the thoughts of _____ except the _____ of _____.

GOING DEEPER

The book of 1 Corinthians is Paul's letter to the church at Corinth, where he had preached during his second missionary journey. Paul had received reports of problems at the church (1 Cor. 1:11) and wanted to address the immorality and disorder that was growing among the people. One topic was that wisdom does not come from man but that it is divinely revealed, as seen in 1 Corinthians 2:11 and the verses surrounding it:

"These are the things God has revealed to us by his Spirit. The Spirit searches all things, even the deep things of God" (v. 10 NIV). "What we have received is not the spirit of the world, but the Spirit who is from God, so that we may understand what God has freely given us." (v. 12).

Paul compares the Holy Spirit's knowledge of God's mind to a person's knowledge of his own mind. Even if you are friends with someone for years, or married to someone for years, only that person can know his or her own mind. Our most personal thoughts, the deepest recesses of our hearts and minds, are only known to ourselves. Only the Holy Spirit, in a similar way, can know the depths of God and the thoughts of God.

The Holy Spirit is divinely appointed for the transmission and communication of God's truth (John 16:13). This revelation is God's pure Word.

REFLECT

1. Read John 1:1. What is the "Word?" Explain.

2. Since the Holy Spirit is appointed for communication, and He knows the thoughts of God, how does this affect our spiritual understanding?

3. Read 2 Peter 1:21. Does this verse explain the unique principle of divine truth versus human understanding? How do we benefit from this? Discuss.

4. Can you think of a time when you helped someone understand something in the Bible? How would you compare this with explaining a math problem? Discuss.

THE HOLY SPIRIT ASSURES GOD'S LOVE

And hope does not put us to shame, because God's love has been poured out into our hearts through the Holy Spirit, who has been given to us. (Rom. 5:5 NIV)

LEARNING THE SCRIPTURE

1. _____ does not put us to shame.

2. Because God's _____ has been _____ _____ into our hearts through the _____ _____, who has been given to us.

GOING DEEPER

God loves us so much that He sent His son, Jesus, to save us, and continues to send His love through the Holy Spirit. The importance of this love cannot be overstated. When a person receives Jesus at salvation, that person begins a limitless love relationship with God that lasts throughout eternity. "For if, while we were God's enemies, we were reconciled to him through the death of his Son, how much more, having been reconciled, shall we be saved through his life!" (v. 10 NIV).

In Paul's letter to the Romans, he assures believers about the security of their salvation and God's love. God's love comes to us through the Holy Spirit, who makes us feel the love of God, and fills our hearts with love for God; we love Him because He first loved us (1 John 4:19). This love is the inspiration of all our actions and the motivation for our obedience.

Paul says we can count on this love because God pours it into the hearts of believers through the Holy Spirit. The Greek word for "pour" is *ekcheo*, which means "to gush" or "to bestow liberally" (Strong's 1632). For those who are redeemed through Christ, God's love does not trickle down, it gushes.

REFLECT

1. Why do you think God pours His love into our hearts? Discuss.

2. Read Psalm 119:116. How does this compare with Romans 5:5? Explain.

3. How has the Holy Spirit challenged you to share God's love? Write down three ways that you can share this love with others. (Examples: rake leaves for an elderly neighbor, read the Bible to a person with poor eyesight, take someone to the doctor, volunteer at church.)

   1)

   2)

   3)

9
THE HOLY SPIRIT

THE HOLY SPIRIT TRANSFORMS US

The Spirit of the LORD will come powerfully upon you, and you will prophesy with them; and you will be changed into a different person. (1 Sam. 10:6 NIV)

But we all, with unveiled face, beholding as in a mirror the glory of the Lord, are being transformed into the same image from glory to glory, just as from the Lord, the Spirit. (2 Cor. 3:18 NASB)

LEARNING THE SCRIPTURE

1. The Spirit of the LORD will _____ _____ upon you, and you will _____ with them; and you will be _____ into a _____ person.

2. But we all, with _____ face, beholding as in a _____ the glory of the Lord, are _____ _____ into the same image from _____ _____ _____ just as from the Lord, _____ _____.

GOING DEEPER

In this verse, Paul encourages us by saying that "we all" will be transformed. This does not apply to just certain people, preachers, or religious leaders—but to all believers. Those who followed the old covenant had "veiled" faces, but through Jesus and the new covenant, the veil is removed and we see clearly. Through the gospels, we have an opportunity to study the very nature of God.

This is also explained in Hebrews 1:1–3 (NIV): "In the past God spoke to our ancestors through the prophets at many times and in various ways, but in these last days he has spoken to us by his Son, whom he appointed heir of all things, and through whom also he made the universe. The Son is the radiance of God's glory and the exact representation of his being, sustaining all things by his powerful word."

When we focus our lives on Jesus, then through the power of the Holy Spirit and over time, we become more Christlike. The more closely we follow Christ, the more we will be like Him: "For in Christ all the fullness of the Deity lives in bodily form, and in Christ you have been brought to fullness" (Col. 2:9–10 NIV).

REFLECT

1. Have you felt the change of becoming a different person as mentioned in 1 Samuel 10:6? Explain.

2. Name three ways that the Holy Spirit can influence your life to be more like Christ.

   1)

   2)

   3)

THE HOLY SPIRIT SUSTAINS OUR HOPE

For through the Spirit we eagerly await by faith the righteousness for which we hope. (Gal. 5:5 NIV)

LEARNING THE SCRIPTURE

1. For through the _____ we eagerly await by _____

2. The righteousness for which we _____.

GOING DEEPER

In Paul's letter to the Galatians, he shared a message of salvation and spiritual freedom through faith in Christ. Paul had spent some time in Galatia and was concerned that the people were falling away from what he had taught them.

In this section of Galatians, Paul reminds believers that we cannot earn salvation through keeping the law or through works but that our hope is in Christ and that we are to live our lives through the Spirit rather than the flesh. Paul then reminds believers that Christians already possess the righteousness of salvation (Rom. 5:1–2) although the complete righteousness of total sanctification and glorification is yet to come.

The hope of glorification is not futile; every Christian experiences glimpses of that glory, the fullness of which we will receive after death. "In his great mercy he has given us new birth into a living hope through the resurrection of Jesus Christ from the dead, and into an inheritance that can never perish, spoil or fade. This inheritance is kept in heaven for you" (1 Pet. 1:3–4 NIV).

Paul shares another message of hope in Romans 5:5 (NIV), "And hope does not put us to shame, because God's love has been poured out into our hearts through the Holy Spirit, who has been given to us."

In Hebrews (11:1 KJV), Paul says, "Now faith is the substance of things hoped for, the evidence of things not seen." Believers have the gift of hope from Christ through the Holy Spirit but still await the final glorification of our faith.

REFLECT

1. Define righteousness. What is the relationship between Jesus and righteousness? Discuss.

2. Compare "faith" in Romans 5:5 to "hope" in Galatians 5:5. Discuss.

3. If faith is the substance of things hoped for, how does the Holy Spirit help us "walk by faith"? Discuss.

THE HOLY SPIRIT FLOWS WITHIN US

"Let anyone who is thirsty come to me and drink. Whoever believes in me, as Scripture has said, rivers of living water will flow from within them." By this he meant the Spirit, whom those who believed in him were later to receive. Up to that time the Spirit had not been given, since Jesus had not yet been glorified. (John 7:37–39 NIV)

LEARNING THE SCRIPTURE

1. Let anyone who is thirsty _____ _____ _____ and drink.

2. Whoever _____ in me, as Scripture has said, _____ of _____ _____ will flow from _____ _____.

3. By this he meant the _____, whom those who believed in him were _____ _____ _____.

3. Up to that time the Spirit had not been given, since Jesus _____ _____ _____ been _____.

GOING DEEPER

John recorded an event during which Jesus was speaking to a crowd at the Feast of Tabernacles and making this invitation. It was during a time when some people were

believers and others were not. The Old Testament mentions "water" as eternal life (Zech. 13.1, Isa. 12:3), to which Jesus may have been referring. In this verse Jesus is also speaking about the full indwelling of the Holy Spirit, which would happen in believers at Pentecost (Acts 1:4, Acts 2:38–39).

However, God did not plan for believers to receive the water of salvation and simply keep it to themselves. Through the power of the Holy Spirit, the love that God pours into believers (Rom. 5:5) flows out to others, impacting those around them.

The deepest desire of the human spirit, expressed as "thirst," can only be satisfied through acceptance of Christ and communion with the Holy Spirit.

REFLECT

1. In John 7:39, why had the Spirit not been given? Explain.

2. What did Jesus mean when He said, "If anyone is thirsty, let him come to me and drink. Whoever believes in me, as Scripture has said, streams of living water will flow from within them."? Discuss.

3. Romans 5:5 (NIV) tells us that "God's love has been poured out into our hearts through the Holy Spirit, who has been given to us." Are there times or circumstances in which you recognize that God has poured out His Spirit so that you can share His love with others? What does that mean to you? Explain.

THE HOLY SPIRIT STRENGTHENS US

I pray that out of his glorious riches he may strengthen you with power through his Spirit in your inner being, so that Christ may dwell in your hearts through faith. (Eph. 3:16–17 NIV)

LEARNING THE SCRIPTURE

1. I pray that out of his _____ _____ he may _____ you with _____ through his _____ in your _____ _____.

2. So that Christ may _____ in your _____ through faith.

GOING DEEPER

In Paul's letter to the Ephesians, he tells believers of the great riches, inheritance, and fullness that is theirs in Jesus Christ. He wanted to make sure they were aware of the spiritual resources available to them so they would not be deprived of spiritual nourishment. The same is true today.

As children of God, it is important to feed our "inner" being (where the Spirit speaks to us) with the Word of God. Although the physical body becomes weaker with age, the inner, spiritual being should continually grow stronger and stronger through the power of the Holy Spirit.

"Therefore we do not lose heart. Though outwardly we are wasting away, yet inwardly we are being renewed day by day. For our light and momentary troubles are achieving for us an eternal glory that far outweighs them all. So we fix our eyes not on what is seen, but on what is unseen, since what is seen is temporary, but what is unseen is eternal" (2 Cor. 4:16–18 NIV).

REFLECT

1. Paul reminds us of the contrast between the physical body and the inner being. What happens to one's inner being (where the Spirit speaks to us) under the influence of the Holy Spirit? Compare that to physical aging. Discuss.

2. What does "fixing our eyes on what is unseen" mean? How does Paul describe "what is unseen" in 2 Corinthians 4:18? Discuss.

3. Look up Philippians 4:13. Write this verse on a card or sticky note and put it somewhere to remind you of where your strength comes from.

10
THE HOLY SPIRIT

THE HOLY SPIRIT IS GOD'S GIFT TO US

If you then, though you are evil, know how to give good gifts to your children, how much more will your Father in heaven give the Holy Spirit to those who ask him! (Luke 11:13 NIV)

LEARNING THE SCRIPTURE

1. If you then, though you are evil, know how to _____ _____ _____ to your children, how much more will your Father in heaven give the _____ _____ to those who ask him!

GOING DEEPER

This verse comes from a time when Jesus was teaching the disciples about prayer, and it follows shortly after He taught them the Lord's Prayer.

As part of His teaching, He explained to them that if a son asked his father for a fish, he would not give him a snake—or if the son asked for an egg, the father would not give him a scorpion (Matt. 7:9–11, Luke 11:11–13). Through this parable, Jesus explained that it is normal for children to ask their parents for what they need and that parents don't give their children things that would harm them.

In contrast to human fathers, "how much more" will God—in perfect love and wisdom—give to His children? Jesus finished His point by saying that our heavenly Father will give the Holy Spirit to those who ask.

For Christians, all good things and blessings come through the Holy Spirit. In Ephesians 3:16–17 (NIV), Paul said, "I pray that out of his glorious riches he may strengthen you with power through his Spirit in your inner being, so that Christ may dwell in your hearts through faith."

REFLECT

1. Read and compare Luke 11:13 to Matthew 7:11. What is given by your heavenly Father that is different? Explain.

2. In Ephesians 3:16–17, what is Paul's prayer for our inner being? Discuss.

3. How could the Holy Spirit be the gift of God that keeps on giving? Make a list of gifts you have received from God, and thank Him for the gifts He has given you and the church as a whole.

   1)

   2)

   3)

   4)

   5)

THE HOLY SPIRIT DISTRIBUTES GIFTS

There are different kinds of gifts, but the same Spirit distributes them. There are different kinds of service, but the same Lord. There are different kinds of working, but in all of them and in everyone it is the same God at work. Now to each one the manifestation of the Spirit is given for the common good. (1 Cor. 12:4–7 NIV)

LEARNING THE SCRIPTURE

1. There are different kinds of _____, but the _____ _____ distributes them. There are different kinds of _____, but the same Lord. There are different kinds of _____, but in all of them and in everyone it is the _____ _____ at work.

2. Now to each one the _____ of the Spirit is given for the _____ _____.

GOING DEEPER

The gifts of the Holy Spirit are not the same as natural abilities, talents or skills—all people have certain capabilities. Paul explains that these spiritual gifts are given by the Holy Spirit to believers so they may be unified in Jesus, uphold each other, and glorify God. Spiritual gifts are always for the benefit and uplifting of the body of Christ. These gifts include (1 Cor. 12:8–10 NIV):

Message of Wisdom	Message of Knowledge
Healing	Miraculous Powers
Distinguishing Between Spirits	Prophecy
Speaking in Different Tongues	Interpretation of Tongues

Faith

"All these are the work of one and the same Spirit, and he distributes them to each one, just as he determines" (1 Cor. 12:11 NIV).

REFLECT

1. All believers are blessed with spiritual gifts. Make a list of the spiritual gifts the Holy Spirit has given you. Consider the things that come naturally to you, such as teaching, assisting those in need, or participating in spirit-filled music.

2. What are we supposed to do with our gifts? Discuss.

3. What is the impact of not sharing our spiritual gifts? On others? On ourselves? Discuss.

4. What do these verses tell us about the Trinity? Discuss.

THE HOLY SPIRIT BEARS FRUIT IN OUR LIVES

But the fruit of the Spirit is love, joy, peace, forbearance, kindness, goodness, faithfulness, gentleness and self-control. Against such things there is no law. (Gal. 5:22–23 NIV)

LEARNING THE SCRIPTURE

1. The fruit of the Spirit is _____, _____, _____, _____, _____, _____, _____, _____, and _____.

2. Against such things there is _____ _____.

GOING DEEPER

This verse is part of a passage about the struggle between flesh and spirit. Paul says that "the acts of the flesh are obvious: sexual immorality, impurity and debauchery; idolatry and witchcraft; hatred, discord, jealousy, fits of rage, selfish ambition, dissensions, factions and envy; drunkenness, orgies, and the like" (Gal. 5:19–21 NIV).

By contrast, Paul tells us that we are not to give in to the desires of the flesh, but we are instead to "walk by the Spirit" (v. 5:16). But what does that mean? As believers, we are empowered by God to progress in our ability to respond to the Spirit's leading, and the characteristics of spiritual fruit will continue to grow in our lives.

Notice that "fruit" in verse 5:22 is singular, not plural—it's a package deal. The fruit in a believer's life is an inward awareness and an outward sign that they belong to God. "By their fruit you will recognize them. Do people pick grapes from thornbushes, or figs from thistles? Likewise, every good tree bears good fruit, but a bad tree bears bad fruit. A good tree cannot bear bad fruit, and a bad tree cannot bear good fruit. Every tree that does not bear good fruit is cut down and thrown into the fire. Thus, by their fruit you will recognize them" (Matt. 7:16-20 NIV).

Galatians 5:23 concludes with, "Against such things there is no law." The characteristics of spiritual fruit are in total harmony with the virtues that God wants believers to have.

REFLECT

1. What is the difference between "gifts" of the Spirit and "fruit" of the Spirit? Discuss.

2. Which examples of this fruit do you experience most frequently? In what situations? Explain.

3. How do you recognize spiritual fruit in other people's lives? Discuss.

THE HOLY SPIRIT UNITES US

Just as a body, though one, has many parts, but all its many parts form one body, so it is with Christ. For we were all baptized by one Spirit so as to form one body—whether Jews or Gentiles, slave or free—and we were all given the one Spirit to drink. (1 Cor. 12:12—13 NIV)

LEARNING THE SCRIPTURE

1. Just as a body, though one, has _____ _____, but all its many parts form _____ _____, so it is with Christ.

2. For we were all baptized by _____ _____ so as to form _____ _____ —whether Jews or Gentiles, slaves or free.

3. And we were all given the _____ _____ to drink.

GOING DEEPER

 As believers, we are part of the body of Christ, having been baptized through the Holy Spirit. We are all different, and each of us has a different purpose and different gifts; however, Christ binds us together with him and together with each other. Just as the physical body has many parts that function together, the body of Christ works together for the good of the whole. No one function is more important than another—all are needed to make the body complete.

Christ prayed that believers would live in unity: "I have given them the glory that you gave me, that they may be one as we are one—I in them and you in me—so that they may be brought to complete unity" (John 17:22–23 NIV).

In Mark 3:25 (NIV), Jesus warned a crowd of the risk of not living at peace, "If a house is divided against itself, that house cannot stand."

Paul says that since we are part of the same body, we should live together in peace doing the things that we have been called to do and being secure in the knowledge that Christ is in control. In Ephesians 4:3–6 (NIV), Paul tells us to "Make every effort to keep the unity of the Spirit through the bond of peace. There is one body and one Spirit, just as you were called to one hope when you were called; one Lord, one faith, one baptism; one God and Father of all, who is over all and through all and in all."

REFLECT

1. What does Paul request from us to keep the unity of the Spirit?

2. Read Mark 3:25. What is a house divided against itself? Is Jesus talking about a house? How does His message apply to families? How does it apply to churches?

3. We all have different strengths. Identify three things that you are good at that could be used to benefit the body of Christ.

   1)

   2)

   3)

11
THE HOLY SPIRIT

THE HOLY SPIRIT SENDS US
AS THE FATHER SENT CHRIST

Again Jesus said, "Peace be with you! As the Father has sent me, I am sending you." And with that he breathed on them and said, "Receive the Holy Spirit." (John 20:21–22 NIV)

LEARNING THE SCRIPTURE

1. Again, Jesus said "_____ _____ _____ _____! As the _____ has

   sent me, I am _____ you."

2. And with that he breathed on them and said, "_____ _____ _____

   _____."

GOING DEEPER

It was the evening of the first Resurrection Sunday. Jesus had now been crucified three days, and ten of the disciples were gathered behind locked doors, hiding from Jewish leaders (John 20:19). They had heard from Mary Magdalene and others that they had seen the risen Jesus; however, the disciples considered the report as "nonsense" (Luke 24:11).

Then to their amazement, Jesus suddenly appeared in the room—providing physical proof that He had risen from the dead. Joy immediately filled the room (John 20:20). Jesus then gave them instructions, telling them that as He had been sent by the Father, He was now sending them, armed with the power of the Holy Spirit, the fullness of which they would receive at Pentecost (Acts 2:1–4).

The act of being sent reminds us of the Great Commission, which states: "Then Jesus came to them and said, 'All authority in heaven and on earth has been given to me. Therefore, go and make disciples of all nations, baptizing them in the name of the Father and of the Son and of the Holy Spirit, and teaching them to obey everything I have commanded you. And surely I am with you always, to the very end of the age'" (Matt. 28: 18–20 NIV).

REFLECT

1. What do you think Jesus meant by, "I am with you always, to the very end of the age?" Discuss.

2. How did the sending of the Holy Spirit enhance the capability of Christ to reach people through the disciples? Through all believers? Explain.

3. There were ten disciples in one room when Jesus spoke in John 20:21. Who was missing? Hint: See John 20:24.

THE HOLY SPIRIT APPOINTS MINISTRIES

Keep watch over yourselves and all the flock of which the Holy Spirit has made you overseers. Be shepherds of the church of God, which he bought with his own blood. (Acts 20:28 NIV)

LEARNING THE SCRIPTURE

1. Keep _____ over yourselves and all the _____ of which the Holy Spirit has made you overseers.

2. Be _____ of the church of God, which he _____ with his own blood.

GOING DEEPER

In this passage, Luke records a time when he was with Paul in Miletus, an ancient Greek city on what is now the western coast of Turkey. Paul had summoned the leaders of the church at nearby Ephesus in order to say goodbye, as he was heading to Jerusalem and did not expect to return to the area (Act 20:17–23). Paul told them that the Holy Spirit is

the one that leads us to minister to others. God has paid for the church through the blood of Jesus, and it is our duty and privilege to give of ourselves to the church and spread His gospel to others.

The word "shepherd" translates from the Greek word *poimainó*, which is a comprehensive term meaning that the shepherd has total responsibility for the flock, the most important task being feeding the sheep (Strong's 4165). Throughout Scripture, there are several instances in which a metaphor for God as a shepherd caring for His flock is used, perhaps most famously by David in Psalm 23:1 (NASB), "The LORD is my shepherd; I shall not want."

REFLECT

1. The phrase "keep watch over yourselves" includes paying attention to what you are being spiritually fed. How does the Holy Spirit feed you? How does that help you to feed others? Discuss.

2. Does the sentence "Be shepherds of the church of God, which he bought with his own blood" affect your view of the shepherd's responsibility? Discuss.

3. Have you identified your personal ministry? If so, make a list of the ways the Holy Spirit is supporting you in your efforts. If not, refer to the gifts you listed on page 95 to recognize ways that the Holy Spirit may be equipping you to "shepherd" others.

   1)

   2)

   3)

   4)

   5)

THE HOLY SPIRIT IS OUR ANOINTING

As for you, the anointing you received from him remains in you, and you do not need anyone to teach you. But as his anointing teaches you about all things and as that anointing is real, not counterfeit—just as it has taught you, remain in him. (1 John 2:27 NIV)

LEARNING THE SCRIPTURE

1. As for you, the anointing you received from him _____ in you, and you do not need anyone to _____ _____.

2. But as his _____ teaches you about all things and as that anointing is _____, not _____ —

3. Just as it has taught you, _____ _____ _____.

GOING DEEPER

John wrote this letter during a time when many false religions were springing up throughout Asia Minor in an area that is now Turkey. While it is not certain who the intended audience was for the letter, it is believed that John knew them on a personal basis. John had oversight of many of the churches in the region, and he wanted to remind them of the truth they had received from him—and to not be fooled by false teaching.

"But you have an anointing from the Holy One, and all of you know the truth" (1 John 2:20 NIV). "I am writing these things to you about those who are trying to lead you astray" (v. 26).

In Greek, the word "anoint" (*chrisma*) means "a smearing of" or "the special endowment of" the Holy Spirit (Strong's 5545). Because believers have received this anointing, the Holy Spirit guides us so that we can recognize false teachings from the truth. Those who belong to Christ have been anointed to receive instruction, guidance, discernment, and "inside" information from Scripture through the Holy Spirit.

That's not to say that we don't need human teachers. Christ Himself has appointed pastors and other leaders "for the equipping of the saints for the work of service, to the building up of the body of Christ" (Eph. 4:12 NASB). John's message is that we should not rely on human wisdom but on the Spirit-led teaching of God's Word.

REFLECT

1. In 1 John 2:27, what has been received? Discuss.

2. Think about the biblical truth that has been affirmed to you through your anointing. Does this enhance your confidence in your comprehension of Scripture? How might that understanding help you with a friend who is hurting and seeks your advice? Explain.

THE HOLY SPIRIT INSPIRES US TO SPEAK

For the Holy Spirit will teach you at that time what you should say. (Luke 12:12 NIV)

LEARNING THE SCRIPTURE

1. For the _____ _____ will teach you at that time what you should _____.

GOING DEEPER

Luke tells of a time when Jesus addressed a mostly hostile crowd of several thousand people. Before He spoke, He warned the disciples to be on the lookout for the hypocritical influence of the Pharisees (v. 1), who were part of the ruling body in Israel.

Jesus told the disciples that the truth about the Father, the Son, and the Holy Spirit would be made known and that the disciples should stand firm in their faith and boldly proclaim the truth about God: "I tell you, whoever publicly acknowledges me before others, the Son of Man will also acknowledge before the angels of God. But whoever disowns me before others will be disowned before the angels of God. And everyone who speaks a word against the Son of Man will be forgiven, but anyone who blasphemes against the Holy Spirit will not be forgiven" (vv. 8–10 NIV).

Jesus told the disciples that if they were arrested and taken in front of the authorities, they would not need to worry about how to defend themselves (v. 12) and that the Holy Spirit would give them the right things to say.

When someone receives a message from God about Jesus, that person can only speak the truth about Christ as revealed by the Holy Spirit or lie from the spirit of the enemy. There are no middle-ground answers with Christ. ("So, because you are lukewarm—neither hot nor cold—I am about to spit you out of my mouth" [Rev. 3:16 NIV]; "Whoever is not with me is against me, and whoever does not gather with me scatters" [Matt. 12:30 NIV].)

It is the work of the Holy Spirit that allows us to confess Jesus as Lord. "Consequently, faith comes from hearing the message, and the message is heard through the word about Christ" (Rom. 10:17 NIV).

REFLECT

1. Think of a time when the Holy Spirit inspired you to speak, pray, or sing. What were the circumstances, and how did it make you feel? Describe.

2. Does the Holy Spirit that resides in you leave you comfortable with a lukewarm attitude? What happens if we remain lukewarm? How might He help us change our attitudes? Discuss.

3. What do you think the Holy Spirit does for you when you are asked to defend yourself? Discuss.

12
THE HOLY SPIRIT

THE HOLY SPIRIT BRINGS GOOD NEWS

The Spirit of the Sovereign LORD is on me, because the LORD has anointed me to proclaim good news to the poor. He has sent me to bind up the brokenhearted, to proclaim freedom for the captives and release from darkness for the prisoners. (Isa. 61:1 NIV)

LEARNING THE SCRIPTURE

1. The Spirit of the _____ LORD is on me.

2. Because the LORD has _____ me to proclaim good news to the poor.

3. He has _____ ____ to bind up the _____, to _____ freedom for the captives and release _____ _____ for the prisoners.

GOING DEEPER

Isaiah was a prophet born in the eighth century BC. A Latin priest named Jerome, who lived from AD 342 to 420 and translated most of the Bible into Latin, praised Isaiah saying, "He was more of an evangelist than a prophet, because he described all of the mysteries of the Church of Christ so vividly that you would assume he was not

prophesying about the future, but rather was composing a history of past events" (*The Lives of the Holy Prophets*, Holy Apostles Convent).

Isaiah 61:1 is repeated (in part) by Luke's account of Jesus reading the passage Isaiah had written about Jesus some 650 years prior to His birth (Luke 4:16–19 NIV): "He went to Nazareth, where he had been brought up, and on the Sabbath day he went into the synagogue, as was his custom. He stood up to read, and the scroll of the prophet Isaiah was handed to him. Unrolling it, he found the place where it is written:

'The Spirit of the Lord is on me, because he has anointed me to proclaim good news to the poor. He has sent me to proclaim freedom for the prisoners and recovery of sight for the blind, to set the oppressed free, to proclaim the year of the Lord's favor.'"

REFLECT

1. How did Isaiah know that he had been anointed? Explain.

2. Who are "the poor"? Do you think we are also called to proclaim good news to the poor? Why?

3. What is meant by "bind up the brokenhearted"? Has your heart been broken? How did God work with you before, during, and after this time through the power of the Holy Spirit? Write down your thoughts.

THE HOLY SPIRIT REVEALS THINGS TO COME

He will not speak on his own; he will speak only what he hears, and he will tell you what is yet to come. He will glorify me because it is from me that he will receive what he will make known to you. All that belongs to the Father is mine. That is why I said the Spirit will receive from me what he will make known to you. (John 16:13–15 NIV)

LEARNING THE SCRIPTURE

1. He will not speak _____ _____ _____; he will speak only what he _____, and he will _____ _____ what is yet to come.

2. He will _____ me because it is _____ _____ that he will receive what he will make known to you.

3. All that belongs to the Father is _____. That is why I said the Spirit will _____ _____ _____ what he will make _____ _____ _____.

GOING DEEPER

In this passage, John records Christ's message to the disciples at the Last Supper. Jesus knows the attitude of each person and his capacity to understand what is about to happen. To comfort them and calm their fears, He tells them that the Holy Spirit will

soon be there to guide and teach them. And since Jesus has access to everything the Father has, He will share that with them also.

The coming of the Holy Spirit was an incredible advantage for the disciples. All the gifts, all the teachings, and all the writings of the apostles would be under the direction of the Holy Spirit in order to glorify Christ. This includes the gospels and everything from Pentecost to the eternal state described in Revelation.

Similarly, through Scripture, the Holy Spirit reveals the truth about Christ to believers, molding them into the image of Jesus (2 Cor. 3:18).

The passage of John 16:13–15 also provides insight into the amazing Trinitarian nature of God, with Jesus saying that all the Father has belongs to Him and that the Holy Spirit will speak only what He hears from Him.

REFLECT

1. How does Jesus explain what is His, along with what is the Father's, and make it known to us through the Holy Spirit?

2. Read John 14:17. What distinction does Christ make between the Holy Spirit while Christ is alive and after He is gone?

3. What does this passage teach us about the Trinity of God?

THE HOLY SPIRIT BRINGS FORTH SERVICE TO OTHERS

But now, by dying to what once bound us, we have been released from the law so that we serve in a new way of the Spirit, and not in the old way of the written code. (Rom. 7:6 NIV)

LEARNING THE SCRIPTURE

1. But now, by _____ to what once _____ us,

2. We have been _____ from the _____ so that we _____ in a new way of the _____.

3. And not in the old way of the _____ _____.

GOING DEEPER

In Romans 7:1–6, Paul explains that believers are no longer under the old law regarding its power to condemn; but rather that believers have "died to the law through the body of Christ, that you might belong to another, to him who was raised from the dead, in order that we might bear fruit for God" (v. 4).

Paul says that having been released from the law and through the power and guidance of the Holy Spirit, believers will serve God in a new way and bear fruit. In verse 6, the Greek word for "serve" is *douleuō*, which is translated to mean "to be a slave to," describing someone whose purpose is to obey the will of his or her master (Strong's 1398).

Jesus was the ultimate servant and explained the importance of service: "Whoever wants to become great among you must be your servant, and whoever wants to be first must be slave of all. For even the Son of Man did not come to be served, but to serve, and to give his life as a ransom for many" (Mark 10:43–45 NIV).

On the night of the Last Supper—as one of Jesus's final actions on earth—He washed the feet of the disciples (John 13:5). This was an outward sign of His love for them, His humility, and an example of how they were to serve each other. Afterwards He told them, "I have set you an example that you should do as I have done for you. Very truly I tell you, no servant is greater than his master, nor is a messenger greater than the one who sent him. Now that you know these things, you will be blessed if you do them" (John 13:15–17 NIV).

REFLECT

1. Can you recall a time when you felt inspired to help someone? Perhaps it was a young person with car trouble, or someone with packages needing help opening a door, or a neighbor needing help with a chore. Did you feel something inside prompting you to help? How was the Holy Spirit communicating to you?

2. Can you use these clues to enhance your daily spiritual walk? Could they perhaps prompt you to think of ways to help fellow believers in their walk? Discuss.

3. Is there a non-believer in your life who might benefit from your example of service? If so, identify an activity that you will invite the person to participate in with you. Write down the activity and when you will extend the invitation. Could God use this opportunity to speak to that person's heart?

THE HOLY SPIRIT WAITS WITH US
FOR CHRIST'S RETURN

The Spirit and the bride say, "Come!" And let the one who hears say, "Come!" Let the one who is thirsty come; and let the one who wishes take the free gift of the water of life. (Rev. 22:17 NIV)

LEARNING THE SCRIPTURE

1. The _____ and the _____ say, _____!

2. Let the _____ who hears say, _____!

3. Let the one who is _____ come; and let the one who wishes take the

   _____ _____ of the _____ of life.

GOING DEEPER

The book of Revelation gives encouragement and hope for all Christians to continue watching for the triumphant return of Jesus Christ. It also warns nonbelievers about the final judgement on the Last Day.

In verse 22:17, two invitations are extended by the two exclamations of "Come!" The first "Come!" is addressed to Christ, inviting Him to return to the world; the second "Come!" is addressed to the world, inviting sinners to come to Christ. In the first statement, the Spirit and the bride (Christ's church) call for Christ's return; in the second statement, Christ beckons sinners to join the Spirit and bride in calling for His return.

Since there are only four verses in the Bible after this one, this verse is a final, sweeping invitation for sinners to repent and come to Christ. The "one who hears" with faith and believes is the one who will be saved because "faith comes from hearing the message, and the message is heard through the word about Christ" (Rom. 10:17 NIV).

The "one who hears" is further described as the "one who is thirsty" with the concept of "thirst" being a metaphor for a spiritual need. John promises that the water of life—

salvation—is freely offered to those with thirsty hearts seeking forgiveness, thirsty minds seeking the truth, and thirsty souls seeking Christ.

REFLECT

1. Identify the Spirit and the bride in Revelation 22:17. Who is being addressed and invited to come?

2. John quoted Jesus as saying, "Whoever believes in me, as Scripture has said, rivers of living water will flow from within them" (John 7:38 NIV). What is required for people to have rivers of living water flow within them? Discuss.

3. Flowing water is the opposite of stagnant water. Do you believe the river that flows within us is a gift God wants us to share with others who thirst? Discuss.

4. Do you feel personally empowered that you could share your awareness of the Holy Spirit with others? Explain.

Index of Scripture